American Immigration: A Very Short Introduction

VERY SHORT INTRODUCTIONS are for anyone wanting a stimulating and accessible way into a new subject. They are written by experts, and have been translated into more than 45 different languages.

The series began in 1995, and now covers a wide variety of topics in every discipline. The VSI library currently contains over 650 volumes—a Very Short Introduction to everything from Psychology and Philosophy of Science to American History and Relativity—and continues to grow in every subject area.

Very Short Introductions available now:

Available soon:

AMPHIBIANS T. S. Kemp

MODERN BRAZIL Anthony W. Pereira

ARBITRATION Thomas Schultz and
Thomas D. Grant

THE VIRTUES Craig A. Boyd and
Kevin Timpe

PHILOSOPHY OF PHYSICS
David Wallace

For more information visit our website

www.oup.com/vsi/

David A. Gerber

AMERICAN IMMIGRATION

A Very Short Introduction

SECOND EDITION

OXFORD
UNIVERSITY PRESS

OXFORD
UNIVERSITY PRESS

Oxford University Press is a department of the University of Oxford.
It furthers the University's objective of excellence in research, scholarship,
and education by publishing worldwide. Oxford is a registered trade mark of
Oxford University Press in the UK and certain other countries.

Published in the United States of America by Oxford University Press
198 Madison Avenue, New York, NY 10016, United States of America.

Library of Congress Cataloging-in-Publication Data

Names: Gerber, David A., 1944- author.
Title: American immigration : a very short introduction / David A Gerber.
Description: Second edition. | New York, NY : Oxford University Press,
Inc., 2021. | Includes index.
Identifiers: LCCN 2020045461 (print) | LCCN 2020045462 (ebook) |
ISBN 9780197542422 (paperback) | ISBN 9780197542446 (epub)
Subjects: LCSH: United States—Emigration and immigration. |
United States—Emigration and immigration—History. |
Cultural pluralism—United States.
Classification: LCC JV6465 .G47 2021 (print) | LCC JV6465 (ebook) | DDC
304.8/73—dc23
LC record available at https://lccn.loc.gov/2020045461
LC ebook record available at https://lccn.loc.gov/2020045462

Printed by Integrated Books International, United States of America

For Chris, with whom I took the oath of citizenship in 1979

Contents

Part III. The dialogue of ethnicity and assimilation

Preface to the second edition

Since *American Immigration: A Very Short Introduction* was published in 2011, much has happened and not happened in the United States to impact public attitudes, public policy, and population movements. These developments include anxieties about border security, which were already especially acute because of the 9/11 terrorist attacks; massive waves of Central American refugees and Mexican immigrants seeking to enter the United States at the southern border; the election of President Donald Trump in 2016 on an anti-immigration platform and, in its aftermath, a hard stance orchestrated through assertions of presidential power toward immigrants, refugees, and in-migration in general; and the further militarization of the southern border. Congressional stalemate over comprehensive immigration law reform continues in the midst of an intensifying, emotionally fraught public polarization on immigration. The political vacuum has often been filled in unproductive emotional and recriminatory ways.

This stalemate is now decades long. The last major revision of American immigration law, which was intended to curb illegal immigration, was in 1986. Immigration, alongside climate change and healthcare reform, marks a singular paralysis of American government. The United States has not been alone in facing such challenges. From the Middle East, Africa, and Latin America, a massive tide of immigrants and refugees from political and communal conflicts has been sweeping the globe since 2010, with 258 million people living outside their country as of 2020. During this period, the southern border of the United States has faced tens of thousands of immigrants and refugees seeking entry, while much of Europe has at the same time faced the same on-rush of people.

These developments make an update of this book timely. In hopeful anticipation of a twenty-first-century turn in the cycle of American responses to immigration, the author contemplated comprehensive legal reform, which once seemed close at hand during the 2010s, as an ideal point for contrast and comparison between the present and the nation's 250-year history of immigration. Such points in time—recurring developments in the evolution of the most significant issues—animate the historian's imagination and make the past especially analytically and practically relevant to knowing the present. While we might be deprived of the opportunity for that poetic rendering of the national immigration narrative, the subject nonetheless demands readdressing, among other reasons because of the need to document both what contributed to the failure of Americans to unite to address it and what has filled the vacuum.

The second edition of this Very Short Introduction updates statistical data and explains relevant events and processes during the decade since the original publication. The choices as to where and how to expand the text, and where to let it stand as written, are the author's alone. So, too, remain his interpretive views, which continue to favor immigration as beneficial both to the immigrants and to the interests of the United States, and his aim to seek a moral and political balance between these two types of benefits.

I would like to gratefully acknowledge the encouragement and patient assistance of Susan Ferber, who has helped me greatly with both editions of this book.

List of illustrations

Introduction: mass immigration, past and present

The United States is a nation of diverse peoples, formed not through a common genealogy, as were its European counterparts among capitalist democracies. Instead, its people have been bound together through allegiance to a constitution, outlining the framework for the making of law and for governance, and a loosely defined, ever-contested creed. Americans are moved to love their country not by membership in an "American family," but rather by the powerful rhetorical formulations of Jefferson's Declaration of Independence that establish the promise of "life, liberty, and the pursuit of happiness." What this inspiring language means in practice is an ongoing argument that holds Americans together.

America's diverse peoples have come from every corner of the globe. They have been brought together by a number of historical processes—conquest, colonialism, a slave trade, territorial acquisition, and international migrations—that involve profound differences of volition and hardly amount to a common experience. Of these processes, none looms larger in the American imagination than voluntary immigration, upon which one resonant myth of American origins has been based. That myth establishes that Americans did not become a nation by accident. Instead, they exercised a choice, even if one frequently conceived within crushing poverty, founded upon their appraisal of the superior American form of government and of the American creed. The Founding Fathers' agreement to unify the thirteen original colonies into a nation-state remains complemented by the choice of those who opted to live in the democratic republic the Founders established and who swear allegiance to it by becoming citizens.

Since its 1789 founding, the nation has experienced almost constant immigration. Especially noteworthy have been three massive waves of voluntary international migration that reconfigured the population: (1) in the 1840s and 1850s; (2) from the late 1890s to World War I; and (3) in recent decades, after changes in immigration law in 1965. Throughout American history, immigrants have been appreciated primarily as an economic asset. Not only did immigrant farmers help populate the interior, but the economy has also had a voracious appetite for immigrant wage labor. Immigrant labor has many advantages as a reserve source of workers: it may fill the need for specialized workers for proscribed periods of time; it may be repatriated or repatriate itself when times are bad; the costs of training and education have been assumed in the immigrant's homeland; and there are not necessarily any social welfare obligations, such as compensation for injury, on the part of the employer or government. In addition, hiring friends and family of low-wage immigrant labor, as opposed to expensive formal recruiting of workers, has enabled employers easily to reproduce a cheap, expendable workforce.

Approximately 35 million of the 50–55 million Europeans who emigrated from their homelands in search of opportunity and material security from 1820 to 1920 came to the United States. Added to that number during that century must be perhaps another million, harder to count accurately, from Asia, Mexico, Canada, and elsewhere in the Western Hemisphere. The first two waves of immigration came amid the transition of the nation from rural to urban and from agrarian to industrial. Immigrants supplied reserves of cheap labor that enabled that transition.

Changes in the immigration laws in 1965 opened the country on an equal, regulated basis to the non-European world, bringing a third massive wave of international migration, for the first time overwhelmingly from outside Europe. America's immigrants today come from Asia, Latin America, and elsewhere throughout the developing world. The epic historical processes that transformed Europe in the nineteenth and early twentieth centuries are taking place throughout the globe. Present-day immigrants are also in search of security and opportunity. However, the trajectories of their histories may be different. First, a significant minority has entered the country illegally, and their position is thus insecure. Second, they are largely nonwhite. Race has formed a principal line of fragmentation within American society and, as such, threads its way insistently throughout the story of immigration. Race separated the experiences of voluntary immigrants in the past, for such visible minorities as the Mexicans, Chinese, and Japanese were perceived as inferior, menacing, and inassimilable, and they suffered punishing political, economic, and social discrimination. Third, the opportunity structure of American society has greatly changed in recent decades, with possible negative consequences. Contemporary immigrants come to an increasingly deindustrialized America, where there are fewer well-paying, secure factory jobs in mass production industries of the sort that once helped propel immigrants into the middle class. Lower-paid and less-stable service, healthcare, light manufacturing, and information-processing jobs make up a relatively large sector of the workforce. In contrast to the earlier century of immigration, when America was a rising economic giant, the US economy has been severely challenged by international competition to maintain its advantage. American workers are often competing with lower-wage workers abroad, and American businesses and industries are vying with more efficient and lower-cost foreign operations.

A source of debate and conflict

Mass immigration has been a source of division among Americans, but the intensity of that division waxes and wanes. Because almost all Americans have their origins somewhere else, they might applaud the melting-pot society that immigration assisted in creating. Yet amid a vast tide of newcomers, they have been deeply divided on whether mass immigration is a benign development, a necessary one, or an evil to be eradicated. Indeed, the effects of immigration on employment and wage scales; political alignments and governmental functioning; schools and other public institutions; the language spoken in the streets, in the shops at the mall, and in government offices; public morality and crime; resource allocation and depletion; and population growth itself all constitute ongoing points of public argument, with nativists and pluralists squaring off against each other. Both sides display little understanding that these issues have been debated before, in much the same terms.

Immigration and immigrants have continually been criticized by those nativists abhorring the culturally and socially disorganizing presence of so many foreigners. Workers, native and ethnic alike, and often their labor unions, have lamented the depressing effect on wages and living standards that, they argue, results from the presence of so many low-wage foreign workers. Immigration and immigrants have continually been defended by those pluralists valuing diversity for its own sake and as the benign essence of Americanism, as honoring the memories of their ancestors, or as a way to find a place in America for their own immigrant kinfolk. They have been allied with employers, who historically have had little concern for diversity per se, but are eager to employ cheap labor. Thus, unlikely political coalitions have historically formed around immigration. The beliefs of social conservatives and labor unions, on the one hand, and of democratic idealists, ethnics, and free market capitalists, on the other, have clashed with one another.

Beyond perennial policy questions, such as the language of instruction in the public schools and the effect of immigrants on wages and living standards, the debate is a forum in which Americans have struggled collectively to define themselves. For one side, the core of American culture across the centuries is and must remain Anglo-American. For the other, the culture continually evolves, with a variety of peoples leaving their mark and the accommodation of difference generating creativity.

The issue ultimately is, "Who are we?" In a world in which nation-states have come to be imagined as communities providing definitions of identity for millions of unrelated, unacquainted individuals, for many that question ultimately presents an existential question: "Who am *I*?" As identities have become more fluid and diverse amid the instabilities of modernity, identity has become problematic. Such questions are overdetermined in the United States, a relatively young society, with a population continually reconfigured by massive immigrations and ceaseless movement within its borders. Many cannot accept the answer "We are everyone." They do not want to consider themselves to be like those who represent, whether on the basis of skin color or of the sound of a language they cannot understand, the antithesis of their ideal image of themselves.

So the debate continues. It is reflected in the shifting character of immigration law and policy. At first, there was little effort to regulate the flow of immigrants into the country, and only nonwhite people—with *white* not precisely defined—were barred from becoming naturalized citizens. Increasingly over the course of the late nineteenth and early twentieth centuries, Asians of a variety of origins were barred because of race, and some Europeans were excluded because of health, disability, sexuality, political belief, criminal record, literacy, or poverty, and finally, in 1921 and 1924, they were restricted through national origins quotas. Then, in 1965, the gates were opened to all peoples, with limits only on the absolute numbers from each hemisphere, in part to appease a guilty national conscience made vulnerable in the midst of Cold War ideological struggles by the racism of past immigration law. Periodically, legislation has been passed to confront the controversy surrounding the vast tide of immigration, legal and illegal alike, produced by the 1965 law. A more comprehensive legislative approach to immigration reform has not been conceived since 1986 and seems distant in the face of the polarization of public opinion.

From the most general perspective, the observer sees that the United States appears to be characterized by the same Janus-faced view of immigration that has planted an abiding tension at the heart of the United Nations' Universal Declaration of Human Rights (1948) and its follow-up statement, the International Covenant on Civil and Political Rights (1976), documents signed by the United States. Both establish in ringing terms the right of people to leave their homeland and to move across the globe, but neither establishes the obligation of states to accept them. At the highest level of humanity's expression of its ideals on the rights of the person, national sovereignty is still recognized as supreme in picking and choosing among migrating peoples, calibrating their entrance to national interests, and creating procedures for accepting and rejecting them at the point of arrival. As was apparent in the confrontations over masses of immigrants and refugees attempting to cross borders in southern Europe and during 2018–19 the American southwest, the sovereign nation-state remains a profound check on the free circulation of migrants, wherever they might aspire to go.

Disagreements over the benefits of immigration suggest that what might prompt a memory of a common or ancestral experience among Americans does not serve to unite them. It is not for want of powerful, potentially unifying symbols of immigration. Consider the Statue of Liberty and its poetic companion, Emma Lazarus's poem *The New Colossus,* written for the statue's dedication in 1886. Both give expressive form to the oral traditions

6

1. After being brought there by ferry boats from the ships that had carried them across the sea, immigrants waited in the Main Hall at Ellis Island to begin official processing by doctors and inspectors.

of millions of contemporary Americans and provide an emotionally compelling immigration myth celebrating America's redemptive powers. It is the narrative of Lazarus's "huddled masses yearning to breathe free." They arrive poor and exhausted, or, as Lazarus, the descendent of Jewish immigrants, would have it in her unpromising characterization, "wretched refuse." Consider, too, not far away in New York harbor, Ellis Island, the nation's largest immigrant receiving center for many decades, a site made into a powerfully evocative legend through the popularization of historical photographs and the skillful marketing of those who saved it from ruin after it fell into disuse in the mid-twentieth century. Here Europeans, the vast majority of immigrants historically, were processed before their journeys to the mainland.

In those photographs, most look unprepared for their American lives, but as popular memory has it, they were hard-working and aspiring. Without assistance from government, aided only by family and through their own efforts to build community solidarity, they took advantage of the gift of American liberty to improve themselves. While they were less welcomed than simply admitted and then encountered many difficulties in resettling and establishing permanence, they prevailed in the struggle for security and prosperity. In the process, it is said, they became Americans, with a powerful feeling of belonging to their new country.

The myth may contain some truth for understanding the majority of white European immigrants and their ethnic descendants. It does not aid an understanding of those not considered white, for their naturalization was hindered at the very birth of the country by legislation that limited citizenship to white people, though that principle was unevenly applied over time, and their immigration was proscribed in later decades. Chinese immigration was significantly limited by law after 1882, and law and policy thereafter badly disrupted Chinese American culture by hindering family formation and withholding opportunity. Angel Island in San Francisco harbor, where Chinese and other Asian immigrants disembarked and were subject to all manner of official harassment, has symbolic implications different from those of Ellis Island.

Nor might it clarify understanding of the lives of thousands of Mexicans or Filipinos who were coerced into returning to their countries during the 1930s Great Depression because local and state governments preferred to support the white unemployed, or of the 120,000 Japanese, most of the Japanese American population and 62 percent of them American citizens, forced into internment camps during World War II. Though these non-European groups found an integral place in American society after 1945, their struggles were especially intense because of racism.

Even for the massive number of Europeans, the story of American immigration is much more complex than self-congratulatory, patriotic narratives would have us believe. While they were rarely greeted with open arms by immigration officials, or by Americans in general, they were nonetheless, often grudgingly, regarded as white in a society where color was a marker of status. However, they were frequently conceived by Americans as if they were members of different races, because race in this historical context often implied not only color, but also what today might be called "nationality." Race often carried the idea that peoples who did not look much different from Americans might nonetheless bear inner, ineradicable, mostly negative traits to which culture and small points of physiognomy were clues.

The processing of immigrants at the point of disembarkation was much less formal before the early twentieth century, but at that time it became impersonal and bureaucratic and was carried out with assembly-line precision. In light of the many millions of people to be processed in the late nineteenth and early twentieth centuries, it is difficult to imagine it could have been done differently. Immigration was an especially important point on which emerging conceptions of American national interest and processes of state power were focused. The American state was coming to maturity through exercising sovereignty at its borders, separating the acceptable from the undesirable entrant, and its efforts combined the challenges of recruiting a labor force, protecting public safety, and rejecting those deemed incapable of supporting themselves, all rendered through the prism of prejudices generated by ideas of race and nationality. Approximately 98 percent of the European immigrants came through the process successfully, while the other 1 to 2 percent were turned away on a variety of political, social, and physical and mental health criteria. In contrast, one-quarter of the Chinese seeking entry were excluded.

Scrutiny at the border was an anxiety-producing encounter, but for most Europeans it amounted to momentary discomfort. Their labor was needed. The masses of working people, especially those from Ireland and southern and eastern Europe, were not believed to be as good material for citizenship and respectable living as the white, native-born of Anglo-American stock, who commanded the public and private institutions of the country and sought to set the tone of its manners and morals. But these immigrants were tentatively, though hardly universally, regarded as capable of self-improvement and becoming partners in national progress.

European immigrants took the country, with its abiding inequalities, as they found it. Their greatest challenge was learning the rules and habits of the new society sufficiently to make a living and, if they decided to stay in the United States (and many never intended to), to attain material security. A society profoundly embedded with racial privileges and disabilities, America was also from the start a class-based society with deep inequalities of power and wealth. Though it made the path smoother, being white has hardly been a guarantee of adequate means, let alone civic equality.

The millions of European immigrants could become citizens, and they then could vote and enjoy other guarantees of citizenship, such as security in ownership and transfer of property—if they were fortunate enough to have any. Native Americans and, after emancipation following the Civil War, African Americans were hardly secure in their citizenship, and the racialized nonwhite immigrants, though arriving voluntarily, suffered formal and informal disabilities that might leave them with no secure framework of citizenship. All these nonwhite peoples might confront severe discrimination in earning a livelihood, even a poorly paid one. The racialization of European groups led to legislation to curb their numbers, but never to bar their entry. Although European immigrants may not have faced comprehensive social and political discrimination, in material terms they generally began their American residence near the bottom of society, not far above the domestic racial groups and the racialized voluntary immigrants. Some did well, but most of them never became affluent. The work ethic of individuals was not necessarily a guarantee of advancement for these Europeans and their children. American history has comprised many types of struggles to realize the promise held out in politicians' speeches and in the patriotic books read in the public schools, but often mocked in daily life. In the histories of American electoral politics, the labor movement, and various race-based civil rights movements, a number of these struggles came together in ways that helped to transform the United States in the twentieth century into a more just society. Often amid bitter conflict, American diversity and American justice have advanced alongside one another.

Part I

The law of immigration and the legal construction of citizenship

The modernization of economies and societies and the growth of technologies of transportation and communication have led to constant movement among the world's peoples, whose displacement in their homelands has encouraged them to seek new opportunities. But people have not been able to migrate with complete freedom and resettle wherever they wish. Nonetheless, societies desiring immigrant labor have attempted to control the flow of people across their borders, especially when that flow seemed to have reached proportions believed likely to create instability. Relatedly, all migratory peoples have not been equally welcomed. Reactions to immigrants based on race, nationality, religion, and culture have commonly led to calls for limiting numbers or for exclusion. In America, law and policy have been mobilized to structure and at times limit immigration. The ideological sources of this evolution are complex. Persisting alongside the recognition of the need for immigrant labor has been nativism, which has manifested itself in the fear and dislike of foreigners and the perception that immigration destabilizes job markets, political alignments, social arrangements, and cultural homogeneity. Popular nativist feeling has always possessed an exclusionist component that invites political opportunists to seek to exploit the passions of the electorate. But nativism need not always be racist or mean-spirited. Those who want the state to limit immigration and access to citizenship may have little against immigrants and instead may be concerned about the welfare of the nation's established residents. Benign formulations of nativism shade off into plausible arguments for restricting immigration to serve national interests. As long as national sovereignty over borders is recognized as the right of states and states conceive of it as their duty to serve the interests of their citizens, immigration policy will remain a legitimate government prerogative.

To the extent that law structures immigration, it also structures the composition of societies. In doing so, it shapes the popular imagination. By barring some people from entrance or from citizenship, while admitting others and facilitating their naturalization, law reproduces populations based on an idealized image of the nation. Law conditions people to regard membership in the nation as intended for some and not for others.

In America, there has always been discontent with large-scale immigration, whether manifested in reactive nativism or in thoughtful calls for regulation or restriction. US history has witnessed cycles of open borders, followed by state action to seal those borders. Over time, parochial, exclusivist visions of the American people have competed with eclectic, cosmopolitan visions. In the process of fighting for adherents, both visions have struggled, as they continue to do, to define national interests and national identity.

Chapter 1

Unregulated immigration and its opponents, from colonial America to the mid-nineteenth century

On the eve of the American War for Independence, colonial British North America had more than a century of experience of voluntary, as well as semivoluntary, bonded immigration. The British Crown had loosely regulated the entrance of non-British subjects and made their right of residence, and ultimately their naturalization, subject to few restrictions, because it was eager to recruit labor. Regulatory policies were applied only sporadically. Pockets of Germans, Swedes, Finns, and Dutch lived more or less as equals with the British majority, who were English, Irish Protestant, and Scots.

As evolved in law and in most places in society, the inclusive policies governing colonial white society, in sharp contrast to the enslavement of Africans, systematic repression of the small population of free blacks, and relentless conquest of indigenous peoples, did not always sit well with British residents, some of whom found immigrants from other nations undesirable and feared cultural inundation. A father of American nationhood, Benjamin Franklin, sharply reacted to the fact that his own Pennsylvania, the most diverse of the thirteen colonies, was one-third German. Of these Germans, in 1753, he said, "[They] . . . are generally of the most ignorant stupid sort of their own nation. . . . Their own clergy have little influence over the people. . . . Not being used to liberty, they know not how to make a modest use of it." He complained that they refused to learn English and that the colonial legislature eventually would have to translate its proceedings so that the delegates could understand one another. But officials in London and resident colonial governors blocked efforts to control immigration. Franklin and others learned that protests were futile in light of what would abide for the next 150 years as the principal rationale for a liberal immigration policy: a land rich in resources needed cheap labor to fulfill its seemingly limitless potential.

When the newly created United States addressed the question of immigration and citizenship during its first decade, it was no less generous toward white voluntary immigrants, though the discussion in Congress was pervaded by some of the same anxieties that animated Franklin's concerns. Added to doubts about the immigrants' capacity for citizenship were fears about foreign conspiracies by European powers aimed at bringing down the new republic, because it might become a model of liberty for their own restive populations. Whether variously phrased in terms of religious or political subversion or terrorism, this fear would abide among nativists throughout American history.

Congressional actions did not focus on immigration as such. It was more or less assumed that borders were open to all Europeans wishing to take advantage of the new country's opening. The most important early law that addressed immigration did so only indirectly and related instead to naturalization. It rested partly on the assumption that without a path to citizenship, and hence a way of attaining secure legal residence and protecting acquired property, few would consider permanent residence. Beyond this, for the first seventy-five years of nationhood the government in Washington did little directly regarding immigration. It limited its role to counting the number of immigrants entering the country and regulating the transatlantic commerce in immigrants to contain epidemic disease and to protect passengers from mistreatment. In the individual immigrant-receiving seaboard states of Massachusetts and New York, however, opposition grew to the arrival of the Irish poor in the first half of the nineteenth century. By extending colonial poor laws, state and local governments cooperated in efforts to bar entrance of those thought likely to become public charges and to deport others. Such regional counterthrusts to open immigration impacted perhaps 100,000 immigrants. Though immigration nonetheless remained at very high levels, the existence of the conflicting purposes of political jurisdictions in a federal system of government created a complication in the functioning of the state that recurred many years later in the fierce contentions in the 2010s over illegal immigration.

The Naturalization Act of 1795 embodied a consensus in Congress on the terms of citizenship. In its basic conception of the process of becoming a citizen, and of the exclusive nature of American loyalty, it would largely govern understandings throughout the country's history into the recent past. (Only in recent decades has dual citizenship, which was rejected in 1795, been accepted in the United States, as it is increasingly accepted throughout the world.) The act stated that after five years of living in the country, foreign residents could become citizens if they (1) had given notice two years earlier of the intention to be naturalized; (2) swore to have completed the period of legal residence; (3) foreswore other and former allegiances, renounced all foreign titles, and took an oath of loyalty; and (4) satisfied a court that they were of good character, believed in the principles of the US Constitution, and were disposed to make positive contributions to the community.

The law was only applicable to "free-born white persons," among whom nationals of countries at war with the United States were barred. Aside from its racism, which was not recognized as a moral or political problem by the Congress that passed it, the law, by advancing belief rather than birth as the principal criterion for citizenship, and by its rejection of ranks and orders differentiating citizens, was one of the most generous of its time. Within a federal system of governance, ambiguity remained about the exact powers of the national and state governments in naturalization. This particular tension was removed after the Civil War with the passage of the Fourteenth and Fifteenth Amendments to the Constitution that, in efforts to protect the civil and political rights of the newly emancipated African Americans and grant them formal citizenship, established bases for the control of the national government. The Fourteenth Amendment created birthright citizenship as the American standard. If one were born in the United States, one was a citizen. In establishing this standard, the amendment would later create a legal situation, deeply resented by nativists, in which the American-born children of peoples, such as the Chinese or Japanese, whose immigration was tightly controlled, and who were originally barred by the 1795 law from becoming citizens, were nonetheless themselves American citizens. The same standard applies, equally controversially, to the American-born children of contemporary unauthorized immigrants.

In the 1840s and 1850s, doubts about the capacities of non-British immigrant populations for citizenship threatened to erupt into a successful campaign to change the approach to naturalization. Though the years after the end of the War of 1812 witnessed a steady growth of immigration, with 742,000 people entering between 1820 and 1840, not until the European agricultural crisis of the 1840s and 1850s did immigration and its consequences give rise to reactive nativist politics. From 1840 to 1860, more than 4.3 million individuals immigrated. The greatest cause for concern among Americans was the arrival of poor peasants and artisans, especially from Ireland and the German states. Many of them were Roman Catholics. Numerous Americans in the Northeast and the newly emerging midwestern states thought their rapidly growing numbers threatened wage scales and Anglo-American Protestant cultural authority, and also, as these immigrants became citizens, negatively impacted partisan political alignments. Some Americans believed the inhabitants of Europe's almshouses were being forced to emigrate. Their passage was thought to be paid by landlords wishing to clear them off the land to make way for commercialized agriculture or by government officials who did not want to provide public relief to starving people. The immigrants were said to be assured that they could resume lives of dependency in America's tax-funded poorhouses. (This type of assisted immigration, which is associated with victims of crop failures, such as the 1840s potato famines, and with the efforts to push the small farmer and the peasant off the land, actually sent the displaced peasants of England, Scotland, and Ireland mostly to the British Empire locations of Canada and Australia, not the United States.) Immigrant ships bearing these immiserated peasants were ideal breeding grounds for bringing cholera to North America from Europe, where it had been brought from Asia through the circulation of trade and travelers. In consequence, immigrants became indelibly associated with disease, a thread running through anti-immigration discourse. In the nineteenth and twentieth centuries, for example, Chinese would be associated with plague and leprosy, Jews with tuberculosis, Italians with polio, and Haitians with AIDS.

Nativist organizations, progenitors of a familiar type of right-wing American populism, formed first among urban Anglo-American Protestant working men and called for the suppression of immigration and the seemingly effortless path to citizenship. These fears rapidly became larger than hostility to economic competition and eventually spread beyond the working-class members of nativist lodges. Part of the cultural inheritance of Anglo-America from its foundation in Reformation-era Britain was hostility to Roman Catholicism and the suspicion of Vatican-directed conspiracies aimed at spreading Catholicism. Related fears of the subversive potential of enemy aliens in wartime had been partly responsible for the passage of the Alien Enemies Act of 1798, which enabled the national government to apprehend and deport aliens from countries hostile to the United States. The triumphalist oratory of an increasingly confident Roman Catholic hierarchy in cities like New York, which spoke from the pulpit about converting Protestants to "true Christianity," helped to stoke this politics.

Under the 1795 law, immigrants petitioning for citizenship had to renounce foreign "potentates," a code word intended to include the pope as well as secular monarchs, but nativists had no confidence that this would protect the nation. Many Anglo-Americans conceived of Catholic immigrants, especially the Irish, as tools of priests. If directed to be agents of the church, there was no doubt among nativists that their sworn testimony at citizenship hearings would be a fraud, especially if the presiding judge were a Democrat, the party profiting most from German and Irish votes.

Yet ending or lessening immigration did not become a part of the national agenda. A national political party, the American Party, was formed to advance the nativist cause in national elections in 1852 and 1856, but its stance disappointed the movement's radicals, and it soon faded away. Its platform revisited the congressional debates of the 1790s, in which the precise number of years of residence deemed necessary to be transformed by practice and encouraging examples into a citizen was a principal matter for debate. Five years seemed completely off the mark for Americans contemplating thousands of impoverished Irish peasants they saw in the streets. Thus, the party's platform rendered its anti-Catholic, anti-immigrant ideology in one promise: if elected, it would extend the time required for naturalization to twenty-one years, the period from birth a native-born white male usually had to wait to be allowed to vote. The immigrant, in effect, had to be born and mature again.

The American Party at the national level was led by respectable, if opportunistic, men, conservative by temperament and ideology, who had no intention of unleashing mass fanaticism or violence. They knew immigrant workers and farmers were essential to

American prosperity and power. Party leadership opted not to reform immigration policy, but to reform the immigrants: with the passage of time they would be exposed to American life and become Americans. While vicious stereotypes about Germans and especially the Irish circulated widely, neither group was racialized to the extent that thoughtful people believed inherent traits made them forever inadequate candidates for the blessings of American liberty. Fleeting though its appearance was, the American Party provides an example of a disturbing possibility: that a national political agenda could be formed around targeting immigrants.

Nativist politics declined rapidly with the crisis of the American union that led to the long, bloody US Civil War (1861–65), in which immigrants and natives fought together, North and South alike, in the same armies, and which thus eventuated in a sense of unity across ethnic lines. But the older themes of nativism— subversion, loss of Anglo-American Protestant cultural authority, incapacity of peoples beyond the Anglo-American core for self-government, insecurity about wage scales, and the like— would never disappear, and they would inform efforts to regulate immigration after 1865. Legislation passed between 1864 and 1917 barred laborers who had signed contracts of employment abroad (1864, 1885) out of fear of the effect on wage scales of contracts negotiated with workers completely ignorant of American conditions: convicts and prostitutes (1875); paupers, beggars, people with tuberculosis, epileptics, the mentally ill, the developmentally disabled, and others chronically ill or physically impaired (1882, 1903) who might become public responsibilities, anarchists (1903), and illiterates (in any language, 1917). In 1906 those without command of English were barred from naturalization. Some of these measures were a plausible response to problems of public health and safety. Under such laws, 1 to 2 percent of those Europeans arriving at American ports were actually denied admission and sent back to their homelands.

But plausible criteria depended for thoughtful implementation on fine distinctions and humane judgment. Although that was never absent completely, the massive bureaucratic machinery developing over the decades to enforce immigration law was not characterized by flexibility. On such questions as what degree of physical impairment left one unable to support oneself, enforcement might be proscriptive. Under any circumstance, many immigrants with such impairments came with support networks of friends and family awaiting them and were not likely to turn up in the poorhouse. It was hardly true, in addition, that literacy was necessary for the tasks that confronted ordinary immigrants. Inspectors often imagined that a woman immigrating alone who could not demonstrate ties to an American support network would inevitably fall into prostitution.

Increasingly, too, categorizing peoples was conceived through the prism of race, which overwhelmed such particularized physical, gender, mental, cognitive, political, and moral distinctions and established what for many Americans was the most efficient, convincing way to determine who might become an American. Under the impact of racial thinking, *laissez faire* in national immigration and naturalization law and policy declined, and the state's role would assume mammoth proportions, often guided by the shifting assumptions of a racially inflected nationalism.

Chapter 2
Regulation and exclusion

The path to regulation and exclusion began in the extraordinary melting pot that was California, newly admitted to the United States after it was seized in the Mexican–American War (1846–48). Isolated though it was from the major transatlantic shipping lanes and without rail links to the eastern seaboard until 1868, at the time of the 1840s Gold Rush, California had nonetheless attracted thousands of Americans and Europeans, Chinese, and South Americans. Their numbers were added to the small populations of Native Americans and original Spanish and Mexican settlers.

The Chinese provided valued labor in the gold mines, on farms provisioning the miners, and ultimately in the construction of a transcontinental railroad line. But in the 1870s, as California settled into a postboom economy and confronted an economic depression, white workers felt their living standards were threatened by the low wages that were acceptable to many Chinese. A movement, inspired by economic insecurity, racial hostility, and political opportunism, arose to end Chinese immigration and force the Chinese to re-emigrate. While anti-Chinese politics had some eastern support, its epicenter would long reside in California. Its principal spokesman was the Irish-born Denis Kearney, founder of the Workingmen's Party, under whose leadership the party did well in local and state elections. A powerful orator, Kearney ended every address with his signature message: "And whatever happens, the Chinese must go!"

Political representatives of the white working class, commonly themselves recent immigrants like Kearney, would be prominent in developing arguments against immigration. Not all were demagogues, to be sure, for arguments that a continual in-migration of cheap labor might have a downward effect on wage scales were plausible. But when fused with hatred for the "Other," the ugly face of class politics was racist. Evidence of that racism is clear in that neither Kearney nor the California labor unions advocated a class-based movement founded on the organization of all workers, regardless of their nativity or race.

Throughout California, the anti-Chinese movement engaged in violence and terror. The Chinese were an isolated, visible, small population. China lacked a government strong enough for effective diplomatic protests against such outrages. It was easy to gang up on them and convenient during election campaigns for vote-seeking politicians to champion the white majority. But there were limits to Kearney's influence. He was not successful in convincing workers outside California that the Chinese were a threat to them. In California itself, union leaders eventually concluded that Kearney's agenda was too narrow to benefit their white constituents, and they resented his power. Kearney did succeed in impressing politicians in Washington with the influence he had attained fusing race and immigration. The call for banning the Chinese gained widespread support, including among other minorities. African American newspapers denounced Chinese immigration as a threat to the precarious economic status of black workers. Congress responded, giving California's white population what the most vocal and violent within it desired: an end to most Chinese immigration and the prospect the Chinese would eventually disappear. In 1882, Congress passed the Chinese Exclusion Act, periodically renewed

AT FRISCO.

"See here, me Chinee Haythun, I'm wan of the Committee of National Safety; and bringing to me moind the words of George O'Washington and Dan'l O'Webster in regarrd to Furrin Inflooince, ye must go. D'ye understand? Ye must go!"

2. The cartoonist seeks to capture the irony of an immigrant, dressed in Irish peasant garb and speaking with an Irish-inflected English, ordering a Chinese immigrant to leave the United States in the name of two famous Anglo-American statesmen, George Washington and Daniel Webster.

until made permanent in 1904. The law was not repealed until the Magnuson Act of 1943, when China and the United States were allies in the struggle against Japan, and Chinese exclusion, an effective point in Japanese propaganda, became an embarrassment.

Chinese exclusion began the evolution of American immigration law and policy, as the historian Mae Ngai observes, into an engine "for massive racial engineering" that sought to use state power to define precisely the demographic and cultural character of the nation. Accelerating that process was the particular nature of Chinese exclusion, as Congress crafted it. The law did not block all Chinese immigration, only laborers. Merchants, students, the immediate family of American-born Chinese citizens, and Chinese American citizens returning from abroad were not barred.

The problem for enforcement was sorting out those barred from those eligible for admission. The effort was often carried out with a ham-fisted brutality or cold formality, especially at Angel Island, where the majority of Chinese arrivals were processed. The presumption of government immigration agents was that all Chinese seeking entrance were lying about their status. To their minds, women arriving at Angel Island were not the wives or daughters of legal residents they claimed to be, but prostitutes imported to work in the brothels catering to whites and the Chinese bachelor population. The elaborate documentation and close interrogation stood in sharp contrast to the mostly perfunctory questioning of most Europeans seeking entrance.

Chinese evaded the law by claiming false family relationships through legally resident sponsors, or they attempted to enter the country illegally by crossing its northern or southern land borders, which were then largely unpatrolled. Chinese American citizens occasionally challenged the operations of the law in court, and they won some notable victories. Within a decade of the Chinese Exclusion Act, the government was facing a well-publicized challenge on these multiple fronts, and it was often unsuccessful. The number of Chinese testing the law was never significant enough to be a true threat to state power, as opposed to an annoyance, but sensationalistic press coverage, often highlighting accusations of crime and vice against Chinese migrants, created panic in the public. Federal officials and enforcement officers felt their authority was compromised and reacted aggressively.

The growth of national government activity and power

Frustrated efforts to enforce Chinese exclusion joined other sources of immigration-related anxiety, including a growing racial consciousness among the white majority based on contemporary science and sensationalistic media; a resurgence of mass European immigration, prompting concern for more effective regulation of immigration, borders, and citizenship processes; the acquisition of colonies in Asia, Oceania, and the Caribbean; and large numbers US-bound nonwhite people from Mexico, Asia, the western Pacific, and the Caribbean. Immigration policy moved decisively from openness to gatekeeping, though the precise application of policies continued to depend on the origin of the immigrants.

The 1891 Immigration Act was an unambiguous statement of centralized power. It formally assigned responsibility for the assessment of migrants seeking entrance to the national government. Congress established the office of Superintendent of Immigration within the Treasury Department to oversee all immigration inspection, including new medical and intelligence testing of those seeking entrance. A bureaucracy, large for its time, took shape around processing at entrance ports and, under the jurisdiction of the Customs Service, land-border security. Its energies were devoted principally to rooting out small numbers of illegal Chinese entrants and the shadowy criminal enterprises smuggling them across the Canadian and Mexican borders.

On the heels of the Chinese precedent, racially inspired proscriptions increased. Additional discriminatory responses to Asian immigration led ultimately to further exclusions. In 1907, during a decade in which the Japanese immigrant population tripled in the mainland United States, from 24,000 to 72,000, not exclusion but quotas would be applied to Japanese laborers in response to protests, especially in California. Japanese were considered less a threat to wage scales than to a white monopoly on prime agricultural land, for they were successful in acquiring a foothold in fruit and vegetable farming. Like the Chinese, they were also deemed inassimilable. Having just won a war against Russia, however, Japan was an emerging world power, so rather than unilateral action, as had been the case with the Chinese, a quota system was negotiated between President Theodore Roosevelt and the Japanese government. Under the terms of the so-called Gentlemen's Agreement, Japanese immigration to the American mainland fell in the next decade by a third. (The recently annexed American colony of Hawaii, which needed Japanese sugar plantation labor and had a Japanese population of approximately 40,000, was excluded from the agreement.) Immigration from Korea, increasingly under Japanese control, was also limited.

In 1913, prompted by the ongoing controversy over Japanese landholding, California and eight other western states, as well as Florida, took action against all landholding by aliens ineligible for citizenship. The Supreme Court declared such laws constitutional. Because many Japanese immigrants had American-born children, they circumvented such laws by registering property in the names of their children. The frustrated efforts at piecemeal proscription of Asian immigration and citizenship ended in 1917, when Congress passed legislation declaring all of Asia (excluding the Philippines, a US colony after the Spanish–American War) "the barred Asiatic zone," from which immigration must cease completely.

In this racialized climate of opinion and state action, confrontations about who was white inevitably arose when those barred from citizenship under the 1795 Naturalization Act contested their status. Lower courts and state legislatures were actually confused about which groups fit into the category of "white persons eligible for citizenship." The federal courts sorted the matter out, though hardly on consistent grounds. Judges never resolved whether the recorded history of the ethnocultural evolution of peoples, or contemporary racial science, with its increasingly elaborate biological classifications of peoples, or popular prejudices would govern the question of who was white. They did rule that Japanese, South Asians, Burmese, Malaysians, Thais, and Koreans were not white, while Syrians and Armenians, whom the United States Census in 1910 had classified as "Asiatics," were white. The birthright citizenship of the American-born children of aliens ineligible for citizenship was nonetheless affirmed.

Federal courts also addressed the racial status of Mexicans, who originally became part of the nation after the annexation of territory conquered in the Mexican–American War. The numbers of Mexicans immigrants increased sixfold between 1910 and 1920, reaching 185,000 at the end of the decade and 500,000 in the 1920s, as a consequence of political instability and agricultural modernization in Mexico. After northern Mexico was annexed into the United States in the early 1850s, Mexicans were made citizens and thus implicitly declared white persons. By a consensual fiction, Mexican lineage was declared European, via Spain, and the indigenous ancestry of many Mexicans was ignored. This served the purpose of securing the citizenship status, and hence loyalty, of numerous large landowners, especially in California. Some were Spanish in origin, but many were Mexican or descendants of Mexican and American intermarriages. A federal district court in 1897 affirmed the citizenship, and hence the whiteness, of Mexicans for purposes of citizenship.

On the popular level, however, Mexican whiteness was contested. The new immigrants were widely seen as uneducated, dirty, diseased, criminal, and lazy. Political agitation to drop them from citizenship failed, but in the 1920s the federal government worked to impede their entrance by increasing a head tax on Mexicans entering the country and by denying visas on the grounds that they were unassimilable and would become dependent on public assistance. During the Great Depression, large numbers of Mexicans, citizens and aliens alike, were encouraged, often to the point of coercion and with the active cooperation of Mexican consular officials in western cities, to re-emigrate. The same program of massive deportations and repatriations also befell Filipinos, who worked extensively in West Coast agriculture and canneries. Another group subject to strong racist pressures, their entrance into the country had been secured, in contrast to other Asian groups, when their homeland became an American colony. But they, too, were barred from citizenship. During World War II, because of a shortage of agricultural and cannery workers, the policy toward Mexicans was reversed. A bilateral agreement with Mexico established the Bracero (Spanish: day laborer or field hand) Program, which facilitated the recruitment of labor through temporary work permits.

Legislators, judges, and immigration officials increasingly sorted out peoples by their presumed suitability to be Americans, as opposed to their desire to work. In consequence, Congress and the courts were faced with an array of challenges in the name of consistency. A particularly pressing issue was the relationships among citizens and noncitizens linked by marriage, which introduced the complexities of gender to those mounting over race. American legislation on naturalization did not originally limit eligibility for citizenship by sex, but gradually the courts determined that a women's status was defined by that of a male to whom she was related. In 1855, Congress adopted the principle of derivative citizenship, which held that a woman's status was dependent on that of her husband or father. A woman who was not a citizen acquired citizenship when marrying an American citizen. A reverse of that situation—the status of a female citizen who married an alien ineligible for citizenship on the basis of race—was addressed in 1907, when Congress decided that she lost her citizenship when she married. Legally, these women were no longer allowed to renaturalize unless their husbands were naturalized first (as by a compassionate act of Congress, targeted at an individual), furthering the link between a woman's status and that of her husband. The loss of citizenship to these women led to much injustice and inconvenience and caused bitter protests. After the ratification of the Nineteenth Amendment to the Constitution, enfranchising women and, in effect, creating a political status independent of men, the Cable Act of 1922 and a series of amendments in the ensuing decade were passed. Thereafter, marriage by a woman who was an American citizen at birth to a noncitizen no longer carried with it denaturalization. Such elaborate efforts to expand state power to classify people by gender, race, and nationality stood in sharp contrast to most Americans' desire for a relatively weak central government. The situation suggests the seriousness with which the electorate regarded immigration and naturalization.

The massive wave of turn-of-the-century European immigration

On the East Coast, European immigrants continued to enter the country in enormous numbers. After the severe economic depression of the 1890s, the tide of immigrants reached unprecedented proportions. Between 1871 and 1900, 11.7 million immigrants arrived; between 1901 and 1920, 14.5 million did. The foreign-born population rose from 5,567,000 to 13,920,000 between 1871 and 1920. The points of origin were changing dramatically. Whereas western and northern Europeans predominated in the nineteenth century, southern, central, and eastern Europeans did so in the early twentieth century. The former never stopped arriving, but the latter overwhelmed their numbers.

This change carried tremendous significance for Americans wary of unlimited immigration, and demand grew to curb European immigration. Behind this effort lay the increasing transformation in both the popular mind and contemporary science of differences of culture and appearance into heritable racial dispositions that served to make assimilation impossible.

The newer European immigrants were different in ways that alarmed many Americans. Many fewer were Protestants than the Germans, Scandinavians, British, Irish, and Dutch immigrants of the past. The majority were Jews, Orthodox Christians of various types, and Roman Catholics, and their presence activated long-standing prejudices and suspicions. The physical appearances of eastern European Jews, Slavs, and southern Italians and Greeks suggested a lack of racial kinship with Anglo-Americans, though these differences were no doubt accentuated by the ill-fitting peasant clothing and poverty of most newcomers. The prominent sociologist Edward A. Ross, an outspoken nativist, spelled out these suspicions when he noted in 1914 that "the physiognomy of certain groups unmistakably proclaims inferiority of type." Ross stated that there are "so many sugar-loaf heads, moon faces, slit mouths, lantern jaws, and goose-bill noses that one might imagine malicious jinn [genie] had amused himself by creating human beings in a set of skew-molds discarded by the Creator."

Another difference was the new immigrants' greater traditionalism. Though they knew enough about the modern world to develop effective strategies for leaving their homelands and resettling thousands of miles away, the eastern, central, and southern Europeans were more anchored in traditional peasant social arrangements than their contemporaries within the continuing flow of western Europeans. It was easy to forget that sixty years earlier, the Irish and Germans especially seemed outlandish and had only gradually given evidence of being successfully integrated into American life. The perception of never being likely to assimilate was heightened, too, by the fact that many of the newer immigrants, in contrast to the often more family-based, mid-nineteenth-century immigration, were single males intent on making money quickly and returning to their homelands.

Racialization of these Europeans never approached the ferocity seen in the popular response to Asians. American nativists condemned the backwardness of these European peoples as much on the basis of culture as biology, even while believing it was ineradicable. Thoughtful people might urge a curtailing of their entrance as a reform in the name of saving America, and yet also be sympathetic to the immigrants' aspirations and respectful of their work ethic and family orientation.

But there could be no doubt about the consequences of such racialized thinking: sharp quotas on admission into the country of these more recently arrived European peoples were enacted into law in 1921 and 1924. In expressing preference and disapproval, the intention was to discriminate. Turn-of-the-century newcomers might have been officially classified as "white," but, as historians have observed, at best they were considered in-between people or provisional white people. By 1920 many long-established Americans believed there were too many of them. Unlike the nativists of the mid-nineteenth century, the new advocates of radical change in immigration law and policy did not have much faith in reforming immigrants, but instead demanded reform of national policy.

The calls for restriction of these Europeans grew after 1890. Emerging at various levels of society, these calls had multiple social and geographic sources, three of which stand out. First, the antiforeignism inspired by mid-nineteenth-century anti-Catholicism enjoyed a resurgence in 1887 with the organization of the American Protective Association (APA), which gained adherents particularly in the rural and small-town South and Midwest. The APA called for state control of Catholic sectarian schools, suspecting them of being havens of subversion. It claimed 2.5 million members in the mid-1890s, but this number soon declined because of rivalries among its leaders. By the time of its eclipse in the 1910s, the Ku Klux Klan, which was originally established in the South to impede the political and civic equality of emancipated slaves, was reconfiguring itself as a national, anti-Catholic, anti-Semitic, and antiforeign (as well as anti–African American) organization. It became a major political force throughout the country in the 1920s.

Second, labor union leaders, such as the longtime head of the American Federation of Labor (AFL) Samuel Gompers, opposed unrestricted immigration, reflecting their members' anxieties about wage scales and the availability of work. Especially those AFL-affiliated craft unions representing skilled workers that were the heart of the labor movement in size, employer recognition, and political power held a restrictionist position. Union members often did not believe the newer immigrants could be organized, because their vision of the future was restricted to family and the related aspiration of many to return to their homelands. To be sure, most of the immigrants were not skilled workers and worked as factory hands and outdoor laborers in construction or extractive industries such as coal mining. This was the segment of the working class slowest to be unionized, largely because of the difficulties of organizing an easily replaced, mobile workforce with a diverse immigrant cohort. The fact that recent immigrants, often ignorant of the circumstances of their hiring, were occasionally used as strikebreakers highlighted for American workers that the newcomers were poor material for organizations based on class solidarity.

Labor's conclusions about limiting immigration broadly paralleled the thinking of industrial employers, among whom there was a growing consensus that the manufacturing economy had attained a supply of labor sufficient to its needs. In addition, influential industrialists like the automobile manufacturer Henry Ford had become more concerned with the stability of their workforce and desirous of encouraging settled habits through Americanization programs and a variety of incentivized job and wage policies. Hence, relative to their past encouragement of high rates of immigration, they became more or less indifferent to the debate over immigration restriction.

Third, a respectable, intellectual, and bourgeois face of immigration restriction appeared in the Immigration Restriction League (IRL), which was organized in 1894 by a prestigious coalition of northeastern academics, national political leaders, and urban reformers. They were alarmed by the growth of social problems and political corruption in the rapidly expanding industrial cities, which they blamed on the unchecked expansion of immigrant populations. Their thinking was also influenced by the emerging science of eugenics, which argued that nations should take steps to protect and improve human genetic stock within their borders. Eugenicists advanced such measures as immigration control, sterilization of the disabled, and laws against interracial marriage.

The IRL did not publicly engage in defamatory xenophobia. Instead, it offered a moderate, patriotic defense of the existing social order and republican social institutions, both of which its members believed could only be anchored effectively in Anglo-American culture. The IRL was composed of men of cultural authority and political power, such as the patrician Massachusetts Republican senator Henry Cabot Lodge; Massachusetts Institute of Technology president Francis Amasa Walker, who had headed the United States Census in 1870 and 1880; and A. Lawrence Lowell, a longtime Harvard University president. The IRL's program was gradually enacted into law over the course of the next quarter century: an increase in the head tax on immigrants to pay for expansion of inspection services; an expanded list of excluded classes; a literacy test; and finally, the capstone of its goals, numerical limitation.

The quota system

The path to numerical limitation, which was embodied in the 1921 and 1924 quota laws, began in 1907 with congressional establishment of the Dillingham Commission. Charged with undertaking a fact-finding investigation, it surveyed the entire field of contemporary immigration and included reports on conditions in and movement from a large number of immigrant European and Asian homelands. Comprising thirty-nine volumes, the final report was issued in 1911. Based partly on the commissioners' on-site inspection of conditions at emigration ports in Russia, Germany, and southern Italy, the report dispelled long-held notions that European nations were emptying their poorhouses and prisons and sending inhabitants to the United States. It contained little explicit criticism of the immigrants and praised their capacity for work and many sacrifices to achieve self-improvement.

The report was nonetheless a mixture of balanced, objective sociological analysis and racialist pseudoscience. It rejected the notion, for example, that the immigrants' children were inherently stupid, in spite of widely circulated data about school failure, and stated instead that both educational difficulties and tendencies toward juvenile delinquency were rooted in the social environment of city slums. It acknowledged, too, that immigrants were less likely to be criminals than were Americans. While it attributed some responsibility for miserable working conditions in many industries to immigrant workers' willingness to put up with employer abuses out of a desire to make money quickly and return home, it placed more blame on employers than workers.

Both in biological and cultural terms, race pervaded the commissioners' findings, especially, but not exclusively, in regard to Asian immigrants. Asians were praised for their work ethic, but exclusion was endorsed on the grounds of ineradicable differences. It treated Europeans through racialist frameworks. For example, the commission accepted the widespread notion that southern and northern Italians were of different races, which was said to help to explain the higher social and economic development of the northerners, whom Commissioner Henry Cabot Lodge called "Teutonic Italians." Nor did the commission necessarily embrace science when it conflicted with popular racialist notions. To study immigrant physiology and intellect, it employed the pioneering anthropologist Franz Boas, who tested the ideas of pseudo-scientific racialists, such as the well-known writer and IRL member Madison Grant. Boas's skeptical conclusions, ultimately based on the primacy not of race but environment and culture, were not consistently employed by the commission in evaluating the possibility of innate differences.

The commission's report endorsed limitations on immigration, recommending as its primary means to that end a literacy test, which was approved by Congress in 1917 over the veto of President Woodrow Wilson. It also recommended development of a method for restriction based on a numerical formula. This recommendation, combined with the classification the commission had done sorting out groups, awaited a time when both the public and political leadership were ready to endorse more radical solutions. That moment soon presented itself after World War I. During the war the government engaged in a massive propaganda campaign to inspire immigrants to enlist in the armed forces and to buy war bonds. But after the armistice, a long-standing variety of cultural, social, economic, and political concerns touching on the consequences of European immigration were heightened by a number of factors, including panic about the loyalty of ethnic Americans brought about by the war; fears about domestic subversion prompted by the Bolshevik Revolution; a brief but sharp postwar recession; race riots and murderous invasions of African American neighborhoods by racist mobs in major cities; and a police labor strike in a major city, Boston, which briefly seemed to invite anarchy.

Not all these concerns could be linked directly to immigration, but together they put the public and its political representatives in an apprehensive mood. Immigration control was one of its principal outlets, especially as immigration from a destitute, politically unstable postwar Europe recommenced. Ethnic organizations and the political representatives of heavily ethnic constituencies, especially in the big cities of the Northeast and Industrial Midwest, argued for continuing the liberal policy toward Europeans, but proved no match for the prolimitation consensus building nationally. The title of the 1921 Emergency Quota Act mirrored contemporary attitudes. The law maintained the ban on Asians and imposed for three years a quota system that limited European immigration to 3 percent per year for individual groups based on their numbers in the 1910 federal census. It limited entrances to 357,000 a year, 45 percent from southern and eastern Europe and 55 percent from northern and western Europe, substituting unlimited entrance with what the historian Mae Ngai calls a "hierarchy of desirability" instead of a complete ban.

When it was found that the law was not achieving the desired effect of limiting numbers, the more radical 1924 Johnson–Reed Act was passed. Beginning in 1927, immigration was to be limited to only 165,000 annually from the entire globe, exclusive of the Western Hemisphere, which was exempted in order to maintain bilateral relations with neighbors and, via Canada and the Caribbean, with imperial Great Britain and in anticipation of the need for Mexican agricultural labor in the West. Quotas were to be apportioned on the basis of the 1890 census, before the vast tide of southern and eastern Europeans had arrived. Each nationality could make a claim to a proportion of the total based on 2 percent

3. Marking the ethnic diversity of men in the US armed forces during World War I, this poster created a model for symbolic representation of American diversity that would be continuously presented in civic mobilizations throughout the future.

of its 1890 population in the United States. A commission was established to determine the exact numbers for the future, and it mandated a quota system that, while preserving the low absolute number of entrants, was slightly more generous—to some northern and western European groups. In total, all of the latter received 82 percent of the quota slots. The new quotas went into effect in 1929, just as voluntary international population movements would begin a sharp decline because of the worldwide depression, totalitarian regimes in Europe that impeded or banned emigration, and eventually World War II.

Between Chinese exclusion in 1882 and 1930, the United States evolved from an open immigration regime to a carefully constructed system that controlled and prioritized entrants, based largely on racialized conceptions of acceptability. The trend in this half century may contradict much that Americans want to believe about themselves and have others believe about them, but it hardly made Americans uniquely illiberal. While the United States was banning the entrance of Japanese in 1907, Australia, New Zealand, South Africa, and Canada were doing the same. The Japanese, firmly imbued with their own notions of racial superiority, banned Chinese and Koreans. While the United States was developing and imposing its quota system, other nations were evolving their own systems of restriction. With the exception of skilled workers, Canada would ban all immigration except that originating in France and the United Kingdom, homelands of its original European settler populations. Argentina established a system of preferences based on Germany and Switzerland, while Brazil did so based on Italy, Portugal, and Spain. When Brazil had difficulties attracting Europeans, its government resorted to the recruitment of Japanese and reconciled a need for labor and embrace of racialist science by classifying them under a newly created category, "whites of Asia." Australia implemented a "white Australia" policy, with preferences for immigrants from the United States and United Kingdom.

Behind the actions of these countries was the desire for greater racial homogeneity, which was widely understood to be the key to cultural coherence and national progress. Through eugenics, racial selection became a basis for improving a population and protecting its gene pool against those deemed inferior, while encouraging the reproduction and prosperity of those deemed worthy to be the majority. When fused to a nationalist foreign policy by the German fascist and Japanese militarist regimes, eugenics became a basis for ruthless war-making and genocide against those peoples and nations deemed inferior. Yet eugenics presented a powerful enough vision of the path to the human future that bitter adversaries, such as Japan and the United States, could share at some fundamental level an understanding of how humanity might progress.

Chapter 3
Removing barriers and debating consequences

Emerging out of the conflict fought to turn back the lust for conquest of racist regimes, World War II was the beginning of a long process of rethinking American immigration and naturalization policy. The revocation of Chinese exclusion in 1943, accommodating an ally and countering Japanese propaganda, was only a few years old when it became clear that the United States again had an international image problem. With the emergence in the late 1940s of the ideological rivalry between the West and the Soviet Union, the United States was already vulnerable to criticism that, for all of its professions of defending freedom, its largest domestic minority, African Americans, lived without equal rights or opportunities, and that in the American South there existed a type of apartheid, enforced by state and popular violence. But African Americans did not have, as did those potential immigrants barred or subject to quotas, free and independent homelands whose governments might take offense at US immigration policy and then become neutralist or pro-Communist. The rethinking of the quota system, however, did not result solely from Cold War politics. There was also a widespread feeling, articulated by domestic ethnic leaders and organizations, that the quota system was an insult rooted in bigotry.

The movement toward immigration reform

The revision of the quota system came in fits and starts over the two decades after 1945, amid vigorous public debate. The first piece of major immigration legislation of the immediate postwar period, the Immigration and Nationality Act of 1952, did not abandon but rather revised the 1924 quotas. Passed over the veto of President Harry Truman, who argued the law sent a message harmful to American foreign policy, it retained the national origins framework, giving individual nations a quota equivalent to their proportion in the population recorded in the 1920 census. The law abandoned the whites-only policy for immigrant naturalization, but it assigned only 150,000 slots to the entire Eastern Hemisphere and provided little opportunity for Asians to gain access to legal immigration. As before, no limit was set for immigration from the Western Hemisphere. Within all populations, preference was given to skilled workers, while the kinfolk of American citizens and permanent resident noncitizens were admitted without limitation in the interest of family reunification. Finally, in keeping with concerns over national security emerging during the early Cold War and building on measures enacted during the tense years just before American entrance into World War II that required the registration and fingerprinting of all aliens, screening of those seeking residence was tightened.

Congress soon found itself forced to confront the massive displacement of peoples on a scale previously unknown, which emerged dramatically in the wake of the Second World War. As many as 20 million displaced persons were homeless and stateless as the result of wartime destruction, changes in borders and regimes (principally the spread of state Communism in Europe and Asia), and decolonization struggles eventuating in the collapse of European settler societies in Africa, Asia, and the Middle East. Approximately 1.8 million people languished in refugee camps run by the victorious Allied powers and the United Nations.

The moral and political stakes were enormous for the United States, which to that point in time had not had a consistent or codified refugee policy. The country had prided itself on being "the mother of exiles," providing residence, sometimes by special acts of Congress, for high-profile political refugees and asylum seekers, such as German liberals who had fled Europe after the failed democratic revolutions of 1848 or, later in the century, Cuban opponents of Spanish rule, such as the nationalist leader José Martí. If the nation that emerged from the war as the world's richest and most powerful did nothing on a much broader scale to relieve this postwar misery, what trust could be placed in its professions of global leadership? In the background lurked the disastrous failure of the United States to do anything on the eve of World War II to address the vulnerability of Europe's Jews before the gathering, murderous force of German anti-Semitism. American anti-Semitism, which reached a crescendo during the Great Depression as right-wing populist spokesmen, such as the Roman Catholic "radio priest" Father Charles Coughlin, blamed Jews for the economic crisis, helped to account for that response to the European crisis, as did the widespread belief that in the midst of the Depression the nation could not afford to extend its resources by taking in desperate foreigners.

Charities, ethnic organizations, and voluntary refugee relief organizations staffed by professionals lobbied intensely for recognition of both the refugee crisis and the ideological and humanitarian stakes involved. Refugee policy directly challenged the limitation strategies of immigration law. The Displaced Persons Act of 1948, renewed in 1950, allowed for 250,000 visas over two years for refugees. Under these acts, 450,000 displaced Europeans, including many peoples, such as Italians, whose nations were limited by quotas, entered the country. The 1948 act favored anti-Communist Christians, including those refugees whose countries had been allied with Germany and had been displaced by the movement of Soviet troops into eastern and central Europe. At a time when anti-Semitism was even more pronounced in American public opinion polls, it was biased against Jews who had survived genocide, which was somewhat corrected in the 1950 revision of the law.

The European bias in that legislation was altered in acts of Congress in 1953 and 1957, shifting the stream of refugees from Europe to Asia. Another strategy for dealing with refugees was devised by President Dwight Eisenhower, who tactically employed presidential parole power (discretionary executive action in an emergency) to confront the problem of finding residences for displaced persons. In 1956, after the failure of the Hungarian Revolution against a pro-Soviet Communist regime, parole power was used to grant visas to some 30,000 refugee Hungarians. After the Cuban Revolution in 1959, 215,000 Cubans were admitted through the same power.

Congress challenged neither of these uses of presidential power, even though it effectively undermined the 1952 law. A strong consensus existed that American global leadership demanded assistance to persons made homeless through the expansion of the Soviet and other Communist regimes. The significant confrontations of the Cold War, such as the Southeast Asian conflicts, and periods of internal instability within Cuba and other Soviet client states put pressure on the United States to absorb more refugees. Refugee resettlement would be materially accelerated by generous government assistance, inspired by both humanitarian concerns and Cold War propaganda-making, which were lacking for the rank-and-file voluntary immigrant. Those policies assisted greatly in the integration of Cuban and Vietnamese refugees.

These cracks in the wall of immigration restriction further inspired the efforts of an emergent coalition of reformers and reform organizations bent on overturning the quota system. The reformers intensified the immigration debate and put the supporters of the quota system increasingly on the defensive. This coalition was composed of elements possessing disparate needs but united around a goal of changing US policy. Largely overlapping with parts of the post–New Deal Democratic Party, it coalesced around a social democratic and pluralist ideology of cultural diversity and progressive welfare state development. Big-city ethnics with increasingly sophisticated lobbying and antidefamation organizations, and liberal Democratic politicians, who represented urban ethnics, were major forces urging immigration liberalization. So, too, were religious and secular humanitarian organizations dealing with refugees and engaged in charitable work in countries devastated by the war. The Catholic Church's presence in refugee and immigration work was and remains strong. Its efforts mirrored both the deep embedding of American Catholicism in ethnic America and the increasing activism of the church in public life that grew alongside acceptance of its legitimacy as an American institution.

It was not surprising to find the lobbying groups representing industry and agribusiness involved with the forces urging liberalization, for they had always equated open immigration with cheap labor. But it was surprising to find labor unions increasingly identified with the cause. Union leadership had long feared the competition of low-wage immigrant labor unreceptive to organization. But in the 1950s and early 1960s the country was so prosperous, dominating the world markets for industrial goods and possessing a rapidly expanding domestic consumer market totally in the control of American business, that a liberalization of immigration policy hardly seemed a threat to American workers. The economy's ability to absorb labor appeared limitless and impressed both business and labor. Many unionized ethnic workers urged immigration reform on their unions. In contrast to their traditional lack of enthusiasm for an open immigration policy, African American organizations also joined the coalition calling for change. The emerging civil rights movement came to understand the quota system as an expression of bigotry akin to racism. A number of its largest constituent organizations sought strategic alliances with pro-immigration reform, white, liberal politicians to advance an antiracism agenda.

The coalition in favor of change benefited from contemporary optimism that stemmed from unprecedented economic expansion and superpower status. The voices of isolationism had been defeated as America embraced global responsibilities, armed with the certainty of the superiority of the American way of life over Communist alternatives. At home, a spirit of unity prevailed, but one that was more inclusive than that evoked by the old Anglo-American–dominated ethos of cultural homogeneity that long inspired nativism.

In the postwar period, amid economic and educational opportunity, tens of millions of children and grandchildren of the second great wave of European immigration took advantage of the widening socioeconomic mainstream. As the economy expanded, not only did wages and salaries increase, but also employment barriers that had stood in their way fell, and new sectors of the economy opened to them. They entered business and the professions in large numbers and gained power and influence at all levels of American society. As they did, their social institutions, such as the heavily ethnic Roman Catholic Church and American Jewish synagogues, appeared less exotic and more like mirrors of American identity. From that perspective, the American melting pot was doing its job well. Slowly and unevenly, the understanding that racial integration was a necessity for American progress was taking hold, as the monumental 1954 Supreme Court decision in favor of school desegregation suggested. It was difficult to believe that immigration could be conceived as a threat to American society. Diversity itself seemed increasingly to indicate strength, provided people secure in their individual communities could unify for the sake of the common welfare. Though they would never disappear, the old nativist and patriotic organizations that had warned insistently against immigration were in decline.

In this mood of optimism and liberal reformism, immigration reformers sought to overturn the quota system. Their efforts culminated in the passage of the Immigration and Nationality Act of 1965, the most important piece of postwar immigration legislation. Yet the public at large was not convinced that any change in immigration law was desirable. While reformist legislation was being debated in May of that year, opinion polls revealed that as many as 58 percent of Americans opposed changes in the law. The opposition, which was represented in Congress by a small coalition of conservative Republicans and southern Democrats, was not nearly as organized as those who called for change. The general public worried that cities would be flooded with new immigrants and social problems; that the ethnic and racial balance of the population would be upset, especially if immigration shifted from white European to non-European sources; and that American workers might face declining wage scales.

Leading congressional reformers, representing constituencies with large ethnic populations, were among the central liberal political figures of the mid-twentieth century. Representative Emanuel Celler of New York City and Senator Philip Hart of Michigan, known as "the conscience of the Senate," were the authors of the final piece of legislation. Its principal spokesperson was one of the leading social democratic figures of the second half of the twentieth century, Massachusetts Democrat Edward Kennedy, who led the effort to pass the legislation in the Senate. Kennedy dedicated his efforts to the memory of his recently slain brother, President John F. Kennedy, a longtime advocate of immigration reform. Kennedy (Irish) and Celler (Jewish), like strong advocates for the Hart–Celler legislation New Jersey congressman Peter Rodino (Italian) and Hawaii senator Hiram

Fong (Chinese), were all associated in the public mind with ethnic backgrounds.

Kennedy argued that fears about the law's likely impact were exaggerated. Countering opposition claims that the intention of the law was to add as many as a million immigrants annually, he stated that the point was to correct wrongs embedded in the quota system and to put admissions on an equal and fair foundation. Kennedy and the other reformers did not really challenge major sources of public resistance. Implicitly, in the minds of their opponents, they seemed to concede that the nation might be better off without mass immigration and with its existing ethnic balance.

The 1965 law passed through one of the most social democratic Congresses in history by overwhelming majorities, 76 to 18 in the Senate and 326 to 69 in the House of Representatives. The law, which took effect in 1968, changed the principle underlying admissions. It abolished national-origins quotas and removed all reference to race as an implicit selection principle. It set annual ceilings of 170,000 entrants for the Eastern Hemisphere, with a limit of 20,000 per nation, and, in contrast to the 1920s quota laws, it set ceilings for the Western Hemisphere, defined at 120,000, with no per-country limits. (These totals and national quotas would be adjusted upward by legislation in 1990.) It created a generous ordering of preferences in the distribution of visas, with seven categories of desirable qualifications: family reunification; refugee status; professionals, artists, and scientists; and skilled and unskilled workers in occupations with an insufficient labor supply. Moreover, a separate track was retained for family reunification, which continued to surpass numerical restriction as a priority in the law. The number of case-specific family reunification visas for the spouses, minor children, siblings, and parents of US citizens was potentially unlimited.

While its inclusive principles made an empathetic statement about the cosmopolitan vision held by Democratic political leadership and liberal lobbying groups, the 1965 law quickly became a textbook case of unintended consequences. Many of the assurances Kennedy, Hart, and Celler gave the public about the likely consequences of reform proved to be hollow. The situation opened a gap between the public and its leadership on immigration that grew wider over the next half century as millions of newcomers flocked to America.

Those advancing the case for reform did so with expectations framed by the dramatic narrative of nineteenth- and early-twentieth-century European immigration. In reassuring the public that the 1965 reform law would not lead to a massive tide of immigration or to a change in the ethnic balance of the country, what Kennedy and others had in mind was that the principal source of immigration would continue to lie in Europe.

The resurgence of international migration in the late twentieth century

By the early 1960s, western Europeans were riding the crest of postwar recovery and had little reason to emigrate. Eastern and much of central Europe was under repressive Communist rule that restricted international movement. It was realistic to assume that European immigration would not reach its previous proportions and that it might largely be restricted in the future to modest levels of family reunification. However, reunification was just about played out as a goal for families separated by the earlier migrations. Over the decades, cold and hot wars and the rise and assimilation of American-born ethnic generations had led to a decline of communications between many Europeans and their increasingly distant American kin.

In sharp contrast, as modernizing economic influences, global patterns of communication and economic exchange, and political instability spread throughout Asia, South and Central America, the Caribbean, sub-Saharan and northern Africa, and the Middle East, vast numbers of non-European peoples came to believe that immigration offered opportunities they could not find in their own countries. The world was on the move, especially to the United States and to western Europe, where both guest-worker programs to recruit labor for postwar reconstruction and the processes of decolonization led to the unprecedented growth of ethnic populations. By 2005, 200 million people lived outside the land of their birth, rising to 258 million by 2020.

Generously allowing for family reunification beyond ceiling numbers, liberal American immigration policy was one of the inspirations for this movement of the world's peoples. Shortly after the 1965 law went into effect, its consequences were seen in a rapid rise of immigration, largely from outside Europe. Immigration totals doubled between 1965 and 1970. Whereas from 1952 to 1970 approximately 5.8 million immigrants entered the United States, between 1971 and 1986 approximately 7.3 million did. Annual legal immigration began to surpass the massive totals of the twentieth century's first decade, reaching about 1 million in 1989, and remained at that figure throughout the prosperous 1990s. In the 1990s, 60 percent of American population growth was accounted for by immigration. During the 1980s and 1990s, only 13 percent of the immigrants came from Europe and 82 percent from Asia and Latin America. The principal sending nations, in order, were Mexico, the Philippines, Vietnam, China, Taiwan, the Dominican Republic, Korea, India, the former USSR, Jamaica, and Iran.

The third massive wave of immigration promised to remake the ethnic character of the United States. By the first decade of the twenty-first century, the descendants of white Europeans were a declining percentage of the total population: 80 percent in 1980, but projected to be 53 percent by 2050. "Hispanics"—the term officially employed by the US Census to describe Spanish speakers

STAY HEALTHY

SEAL OF THE
CITY OF BUFFALO

← 6' FT. →

PLEASE MAINTAIN APPROX. SIX FEET

အိၣ်စီၤစုၤလီၢ်သး ၆ ပျိၢ်

Tafadhari acheni mita mbili katika mtu na mwenzake

कृपया छ फीट टाढा रहनुहोस्।

6 taako kalafogaada

ابق على بعد ٦ اقدام

Manténgase a un mínimo de seis (6) pies de los demás

ခြောက်ပေ အကွာမှနေပါ

দয়া করে ৬ ফুট দূরত্ব বজায় রাখুন

4. The widening twenty-first-century mainstream is apparent in the recent civic mobilizations to combat the coronavirus pandemic in 2020. The languages of this instructional sign—top to bottom, Karen, Swahili, Nepali, Somali, Arabic, Spanish, Burmese, and Bengali—represent the non-European and Latin American diversity of today's immigrants and refugees.

whose origins lie in South and Central America, the Caribbean, and Mexico—were the fastest-growing segment of the population and supplanted African Americans as the nation's largest minority group. Hispanics, only 6.4 percent of Americans in 1980, are likely to be about 25 percent in 2050.

The third wave's social and economic effects have been hotly debated. Urban crime and social problems associated with immigration have not nearly approached the dimensions that alarmists projected. A number of studies have shown convincingly that voluntary immigrants are less likely to commit crimes or to be incarcerated than native-born Americans. In 2000, as the debate heated up, the incarceration rate among men aged eighteen to thirty-nine, the large majority of the prison population, was five times greater for natives (3.5 percent) than for immigrants (0.7 percent). In California, the state with the largest immigrant population, it was eleven times greater for the same age cohort. Other studies have revealed that urban crime actually declines with an influx of voluntary immigrants. Even if greatly exaggerated by the growing ranks of the new restrictionists, however, there are enough immigrant-related social problems to mock the promises of the mid-1960s reformers. Meanwhile, the specter of immigrant crime, especially when fused to the emotional issue of illegal immigrants, for whom data on the incidence of criminal behavior is by the nature of this population difficult to gather and inconsistent, remains a tempting political issue. While the most common lawbreaking among illegal immigrants involves traffic offenses, there have been serious felonies committed by the undocumented, but the extent of their presence among those in the country illegally does not seem significant enough for crime to be the lens through which illegal immigration is analyzed.

Economists have been engaged in a debate for years about whether immigrants are taking Americans' jobs or, in contrast, fill gaps in the workforce at every level in white- and blue-collar sectors. Data on the contribution of immigrants to the economy carefully gathered by the Immigration Policy Center have charted evidence of the multiple ways in which immigrants are vital to prosperity—as consumers, business owners, and workers. Moreover, through the taxes they pay, immigrants also make contributions that prop up the pension and medical programs of the American welfare state. These contributions are especially crucial at a time when the native-born American population is aging, has left the workforce, does not contribute proportionately to tax revenues, and requires such programs to maintain its quality of life in retirement.

Another material benefit of immigration is observed in deindustrialized cities, in which immigrants have been a source of renewal amid the exodus of both industry and jobs and the suburbanization of more affluent, native-born residents. Immigrant entrepreneurs running small commercial businesses and factories are attracted to the decaying inner-city neighborhoods where the cost of buying or renting property is low. In the process, they have helped to renew many large cities.

Yet public opinion is not focused on debates among economists or underlying positive trends as much as street-level perceptions of daily realities. Weakened by global competition and deindustrialization over the last four decades, the economy has not been able to deliver the ready access to opportunity that has constituted the American Dream. Immigrants are a convenient target for resultant anxieties, frustrations, and hopelessness, especially in former one-industry factory towns and small cities that long ago saw the bulk of their jobs move to offshore destinations.

The growth of illegal immigration

The rise in legal immigration brought unanticipated and, for many, troubling consequences. But it was achieved through the processes of law and attributable to a desire for fairness, within a framework defined, if inadequately, by calculations of national interest and national sovereignty. The same could not be said of a more difficult problem that indirectly emerged out of the 1965 law: massive flows of illegal immigration, particularly in its most dramatic form across the long, porous southern border. By the plausible policy of setting an annual ceiling of 120,000 for Western Hemisphere immigration, the 1965 law had ensured a paucity of slots for the rapidly growing population of Mexico, which has the mix of structural problems that have long accompanied urbanization, industrialization, and the commercialization of agriculture. The vast differentials in social and economic development between the two neighbors guaranteed that Mexican immigration, legal and illegal alike, was certain to attain large numbers and be greater than that of any other individual group. The 1970s and 1980s witnessed a large enough tide of illegal immigration across the southern border to occasion the last significant revision of the immigration laws. The Immigration Reform and Control Act of 1986 penalized knowingly hiring illegal immigrants and legalized the status of most illegal immigrants who had arrived in the country before 1982.

But it was not only the magnet of a more prosperous United States that led to a vast swelling of Mexican illegal migrants. Immigration was also a result of international economic planning. The implementation in 1994 of the North American Free Trade Agreement (NAFTA), which was intended to reduce trade barriers between Canada, the United States, and Mexico, continued the century-long quest by Mexican economic policymakers to decimate the ranks of agricultural labor and small cultivators in Mexican agriculture. It enabled cheap imports of corn and beans, the main crops of Mexican farmers, from the United States. Mexican planners, partisans of contemporary neoliberal global economic theories, opted for an agreement that would not only lower the domestic price of food, but also free up vast numbers of rural workers for the emerging urban-industrial sector. The effects of NAFTA were devastating. Monthly incomes of self-employed Mexican farmers fell from 1,959 pesos a month in 1991 to 228 pesos in 2003. Like the beleaguered European peasants of the past, faced with the same relentless modernization of agriculture, the response was not to be herded into nearby factories, but to seek work that could finance remaining on the land. Immigration, legal and illegal alike, across the southwestern border increased dramatically in the wake of NAFTA. In the 1990s it was estimated that between 500,000 and 1 million Mexicans were illegally crossing the border annually. They constituted up to 60 percent of the total of Mexican immigration. Of the perhaps the 10.5 to 13 million illegal immigrants in 2020, just over half are estimated to be Mexican, joined eventually after 2010 by smaller streams of Central Americans (14 percent), fleeing violence by criminal gangs and chronic economic underdevelopment and poverty in El Salvador, Guatemala, and Honduras, where American intervention in past civil wars in the name of anti-Communism had helped to devastate an already impoverished socioeconomic infrastructure.

Many of these Mexican men and women were multiple border-crossers, who regularly earned wages in the United States, went home to assist their families, and later returned to the United States. An underground commerce in guiding those who wished to jump the border gave rise to ruthless criminal syndicates specializing in smuggling people. Behind this movement of people desperate enough to cross the punishing southwestern deserts was the growing dependence not only of Mexicans on America, but also of American employers on low-wage, unauthorized immigrant labor. In industries such as agriculture, landscape gardening, construction, meatpacking, garment manufacture, and light manufacturing, this was observed first in the Southwest and then increasingly throughout the country. By the relatively prosperous mid-1990s, states with expanding job markets such as Georgia or Minnesota, which had rarely seen Mexican immigrants before, had significant communities of both legal and illegal Mexican immigrants.

The problem of illegal immigration was not new. Both Chinese exclusion and the 1924 quota law caused a rapid rise in illegal entries across the northern and southern borders, complete with an underground commerce in human smuggling. Although the United States Border Patrol was created in 1924 largely in response to the need to restrict the smuggling of liquor into the country during Prohibition, immigration control soon became a vital part of the new agency's duties. The response was tougher law enforcement not only at the borders but throughout the nation, stricter penalties for violators, and ultimately deportations, which rose from 2,700 in 1920 to 39,000 in 1929. Yet the policy was implemented unevenly. Regulations were developed to suspend deportations and regularize the status of illegal entrants in individual cases, especially in cases of family hardship. Canadians and Europeans frequently benefitted from these normalizing procedures. In contrast, Mexicans, who emerged in popular lore as the stereotypical border-jumpers, were dealt with harshly through deportations, especially during the Great Depression, when the scarcity of employment led to widespread protests against Mexican migrants, including among Mexican American citizens. In the midst of a postwar boom in southwestern agriculture, illegal immigration of Mexican laborers would spike, even in the midst of the Bracero Program. In 1954 the Eisenhower administration initiated "Operation Wetback" (referring to the short swim across the Rio Grande River that was falsely believed to be the major route of these workers), under which some 1 million Mexican agricultural workers were deported in 1954.

The differences between this situation and that emerging after 1965 were the greatly increased volume of those illegally crossing the border and the heightened anxieties about border security that arose with, first, the Cold War and later, especially after 9/11, the threat of international terrorism. Beginning in the mid-1970s, illegal immigration became a significant, emotional issue, especially in border areas. Though lawbreaking to enter the country to work raised complicated political, economic, and moral issues, it was not long before both legal and illegal immigration would merge as part of a single problem—the presence of too many foreign residents—for advocates of a new restrictionism. In the late twentieth century the nation entered its third great public immigration debate.

The resurgence of controversy and debate

Beginning in 1979, with the organization of the Federation for American Immigration Reform, a number of neo-restrictionist organizations advocated a program that combined a reduction in the numbers of authorized immigrants, stronger border control, and penalties for employers hiring unauthorized immigrants. Public discussion once more focused on protection of living standards and wage scales, crime control, national security, and safeguarding the ethnic composition of the nation as it had stood at mid-century. Added to this was a new concern: environmental degradation that accompanied population growth, much of that growth accounted for by immigration. This issue contributed to the presence of some environmentalists among the new restrictionists.

The tone of the contemporary restrictionist campaign varied greatly. It is possible to argue about immigration in terms of national interests, completely independent of judgments on the character of contemporary immigrants, and a number of individuals and organizations have done so. But the old nativist arguments that judged the character of the immigrants to be defective inevitably came into play. At the fringe of the new restrictionism were radical white nationalist groups, such as various factions of the Ku Klux Klan, American Nazis, and armed civilian border vigilantes, all of whom maintained that the nation was at war on its southern border and employed racist imagery to assert that a vulnerable white America would succumb to invading brown hordes.

Also familiar were the forces supporting the post-1965 policy regime. While not necessarily defending lawbreaking, they supported the unauthorized immigrant, whom they viewed, in direct contrast to the image held by many restrictionists, not as a criminal, but as a hard-working individual, desperate for opportunity. Among the members of the antirestrictionist movement were ethnic organizations, especially those representing Mexicans, who united in response to the extremity of the language they heard from racists and nativists. Legal immigrants have been concerned that family reunification remains a key principle of American law, and many of the workers in the country illegally had family and kin living legally in the country. Allied with ethnic organizations were church and humanitarian organizations of the type that had supported the 1965 reform law. Also, employers of immigrant labor, legal and illegal, argued that in an age of global competition, rising costs, and unstable profit margins, they could not stay in business unless they took advantage of the cheapest labor they could find. Representing the massive California landscaping industry at congressional hearings in the mid-1980s, a spokeswoman for the lobbying organization stated frankly that the companies she represented were dependent on illegal immigrant labor and were doomed to go out of business if they had to pay competitive wages.

Statements of this type impressed labor union leaders with the fact that employers were going to use illegal immigrants to depress wages scales. Segments of the labor movement, realizing the futility of expecting that recent immigrants were going to go away or be sent home, moved tentatively to unionize them. Employers and unions found themselves in a tenuous alliance. Whatever direction groups came from in defending these immigrants, they could all point to studies showing the enormous contribution in taxes, economic output, and consumer expenditures they made.

If the forces arrayed in defense of illegal immigrants mostly looked familiar, their arguments have carried the mark in two ways of an emerging global consciousness that fundamentally challenged the logic of national interests, on which immigration policy had long been formed. First, they argued that the global imbalance of power and wealth, by which Mexico was poor and underdeveloped and its northern neighbor was among the richest countries in the world, required special American efforts to assist Mexican immigrants through, for example, a revitalized system of work permits. Second, in their defense of illegal immigration, antirestrictionists sometimes walked a fine line between humanitarian concerns and indifference to lawbreaking. In embracing the former argument, they challenged the concept of national sovereignty that enabled a state to define its own interests in immigration policy. They argued for a global standard of human rights that encompassed not only the right to leave one's homeland, but also the right to go elsewhere to find work, setting aside completely the issue of whether one intended to stay and change loyalties. In the late twentieth century these views gain plausibility, because national sovereignty had ceded some ground to an emerging global economic system. The ease of international population and capital movements in a globalized market for labor and investment led increasingly to the legal recognition in many countries, whether immigrant-sending or immigrant-receiving, of dual citizenship. Moreover, developing labor-exporting countries hoped to interest their emigrants in eventually returning home with their savings and skills. The United States, which had long insisted on the complete renunciation of other loyalties in its naturalization process, began in the 1970s to accept dual citizenship.

Questioning the principle of national sovereignty opened the way for inquiry into how to compute the moral calculus of gain and

5. Proposed legislation to criminalize illegal immigration led to large street protests in San Francisco in the 1990s. In urging freedom for the movement of those seeking opportunity, the protesters often challenged the logic of national sovereignty that has legitimized the exclusive control by states over their international borders.

loss in rethinking twenty-first-century immigration policy. In the minds of antirestrictionists, what seemed transparent to restrictionists—that unauthorized aliens were at some level criminals—was not a pressing issue. For antirestrictionists, the restrictionists' "illegal immigrant" was instead an "undocumented worker" or "unauthorized immigrant"—terms that referred to the fact that, since 1924, one had to receive, at a consular office outside the country, a visa to enter the United States with the intention of staying beyond a certain time and working. No wonder that in an increasingly polarized, bitter debate, observers perceived the two sides as arguing past one another.

Action by Congress to confront the multiple unintended consequences of the change in law and policy in 1965 did not deviate greatly from past approaches. Yet behind congressional responses to the gathering sense of an immigration crisis and

6. Radicalized by the decades-long political impasse in addressing increasing numbers of undocumented immigrants, supporters of President Donald Trump in San Diego, California, targeted illegal immigration and, relatedly, the porous southwestern border in a 2017 demonstration.

legislative impotence in dealing with it was an increasingly alarmed, angry public. Throughout the 1980s, as the economy went into and then began tentatively to emerge from the worst postwar recession up to that time, polling revealed overwhelming majorities for sanctions against employers hiring illegal immigrants (77 percent) and for halting all immigration when unemployment reached more than 5 percent (66 percent). These numbers remained constant throughout the decade. In 1995 American public opinion stood fifth in the world (62.3 percent) in the number of people wanting prohibition or restriction of immigration. Proof that immigration was becoming a worldwide concern, however, is suggested by the fact that the figure was even higher in the Philippines, Taiwan, South Africa, and Poland, which were themselves also exporters of people, generally educated and skilled citizens seeking well-paying employment.

Legislation in 1978, 1986, 1990, and 1996 veered in different directions simultaneously, as if policymakers were overwhelmed by the moral, societal, and international dimensions of the problem and by the need to please bitterly contending segments of the American public. Alternately legislated were quota expansions, numerical limitations (while preserving family reunification), amnesty for unauthorized immigrants, penalties for employers of unauthorized immigrants, expansion of the number of visas for technical and skilled workers, and increased funds for border control and expanded deportation measures for illegal entrants. The plausibility of seeing the problem as a law-enforcement issue seemed to grow after 9/11, when the Bush administration began to militarize the southern border and erect an imposing fence across the more well-traveled border-jumping routes. Deportations of illegal immigrants grew dramatically during the first three years of the Obama administration (2009–2011), to about 1.18 million. Under Donald Trump, who made get-tough immigration and refugee control a major promise of his 2016 quest for the presidency, they remained at high levels (275,000 per year) in 2017–19. Prior to suspension of immigration during the 2020 pandemic, arrests for illegal entry rose, creating a backlog in immigration courts. In the context of a deep partisan impasse in Congress, both Obama and Trump depended on such executive actions to further their immigration initiatives.

Even before addressing the southern border, in 2017, through an executive order (extended early in 2020), the Trump administration banned most immigrants and refugees from some predominantly Muslim states in Africa, the Middle East, and Central Asia, an unprecedented massive deselection based on religion, in the name of national security. It would also cut legal immigration visas and refugee admissions. Trump addressed the southern border with further militarization and a significant extension of the border fence. He placed political and economic pressure on Mexico to disperse its citizens and Central Americans approaching or gathering in massive numbers at the border.

7. Fears for national security after September 11, 2001, and hostility to the massive evasion of immigration laws on the border with Mexico led to the building of a fence over well-traveled, unauthorized border-crossing routes. Few have believed it is a solution to the problem of illegal immigration.

Those apprehended crossing the border without visas during the period of efforts at mass entry by desperate migrants in 2019 were placed in detention camps, often under chaotic and unsanitary conditions, and family members were incarcerated and many separated in different locations, including small children separated from their parents. Illegal immigration has shown signs of declining from its peak in 2006–7 amid these draconian measures, but these actions are surely not a prelude to the end of the problem. Millions of the undocumented remained in the country, family networks of mutual support spanned the borders, and the conditions of poverty, crime, and violence south of the border that made staying put in one's country even worse than a hostile reception in the United States remained.

The large number of deportations throughout the 2010s and the harsh repression of the Trump administration met with strong opposition in localities around the country. Unable to move either the national legislature or the chief executive toward an amnesty policy and an agreement with Mexico on a new Bracero-type program based on temporary visas, the friends of undocumented immigrants—ethnic and humanitarian organizations and political leaders in constituencies with large numbers of Mexican citizens—opted for peripheral campaigns to oppose the actions of the federal state. They urged local and state governments to become "sanctuary cities" by refusing to cooperate in rounding up and deporting undocumented immigrants, many of whom were long resident in the United States, were well employed, owned property, and had American-born children. Another tactic was to urge upon state lawmakers approval of granting driver's licenses to illegal residents, thus providing a back channel to a document giving legitimacy to claims of residence.

The central symbol of resistance was presented by the claims of the "Dreamers," the approximately 700,000 (in 2020) children of illegal immigrants born abroad, the large majority in Mexico, and brought into the United States when they were young. On their behalf, President Obama announced in 2012 the Deferred Action for Childhood Arrivals (DACA) policy. While it was neither a general amnesty nor an immediate path to citizenship, DACA did allow these individuals, many now adults, to receive a renewable two-year period of freedom from deportation and eligibility for a work permit, if they were without criminal records. Under DACA, citizenship lay at the end of a long, winding process. When Obama sought to expand the program in 2014, he was opposed by a number of individual states and in Congress. In 2017 Trump announced a plan to phase out DACA, raising the threat of deportations, but allowed Congress a grace period to pass what had become known as the Dream Act, embodying the principles of DACA and creating a path to citizenship. Congress failed to reach a legislative remedy, however, and the matter remained at an impasse until 2020, when the Supreme Court ruled that while Trump's Department of Homeland Security had the constitutional power to end DACA, its process for doing so was "arbitrary and capricious" and lacked concern for its effects upon hundreds of thousands of immigrant residents. Meanwhile, Dreamers, who have lived wholly within the United States, the only life they know, continue an anxious, shadow existence that makes education and employment advancement tenuous.

8. Representing 400,000 members in twenty states in 2018 and led by young Hispanic activists, the group United We Dream (Unidos Soñamos) has presented the case for the Dreamers, undocumented individuals who were brought to the United States as children.

The contradictory directions of policy and legislation are evidence of the complexity of the problem that a world on the move has created for lawmakers and law enforcers. In the first decades of the twenty-first century, neither American political party was willing to directly take on the multiple policy challenges associated with a comprehensive approach to immigration. Debates over public policy continued, but the political risks of moving forward, in the midst of the polarization of articulate opinion blocs and the anger of much of the general public, were plausibly interpreted as enormous.

Part II

Emigration and immigration: international migrants' perspectives

International population movements appear at first glance to be composed of an inchoate mass of uprooted victims who have been driven from their homes to destinations for which they are unprepared. The proliferation of modernizing forces throughout the globe has certainly had disruptive consequences, undermining the economic and social foundations of accustomed ways of life. But these same forces have created opportunities promising enough to lead many to consider permanently changing their residence. This section is devoted to understanding immigration and resettlement from the perspectives of the people within these massive migration cohorts, which are defined not simply by nation, but by networks formed out of family and kin, friends, and community. Tens of millions of individual stories are united when the purposefulness of voluntary international migration is considered from the perspective of such networks.

To be sure, migration is seldom an easy choice, and it has often been made within a calculus of narrow, difficult options that carry risks and lifelong implications. Immigrants must be active agents, engaged in strategic planning about the use of the resources they possess that can be mobilized to accomplish movement across oceans and resettlement in new societies.

In the nineteenth and early twentieth centuries, during the classic era of European immigration to the United States, people fused together social and cultural resources to expedite immigration. Characteristics of modernizing change such as mass literacy; cheap, mass-produced publications; and state postal systems that made possible the inexpensive exchange of letters over vast distance were resources in acquiring the practical knowledge of alternatives to the limited prospects available at home. Personal letters facilitated the forging of migration chains. In them, the pioneers of an immigration flow might encourage others to follow them and often materially assisted their passage. Postal exchange also facilitated sending remittances back to the homeland to help one's family. As literacy expanded and popular print culture arose to satisfy the thirst for reading matter, newspapers and guidebooks offered knowledge of the world.

Far from breaking down under the impact of large, disruptive, modernizing transformations, family and communal relationships were key to the ways in which international migration was consciously, strategically organized by individuals in the absence of assistance by governments and elites. Fused with electronic media of communication and exchange, personal relationships continue to be the means by which long-distance movement is organized. What the personal letter once was in facilitating the exchange of information and money among emigrants and their family, kin, and friends, email, mobile phones and video chatting, texting, social media, and global electronic banking services are in the twenty-first century.

Dissemination of knowledge about American life across Europe and Asia and the links that enabled travel to the United States in the nineteenth and early twentieth centuries were products of the gradual extension of trade and transportation between continents. Today, American cultural influences pervade the imaginations of people throughout the world long before they consider immigration. A tightly knit web of communications and transportation already exists across the globe, facilitating the movement of people and information everywhere.

Social, cultural, and economic forces that have provided foundations for international migration, like legal systems that have been developed to regulate it, explain what has constrained and facilitated long-distance population movements. But they do not answer such questions as: Who has emigrated? Why have people chosen one local destination over another? Have they intended permanent or temporary resettlement? Answers to such questions underscore the nature of international migration as a purposeful activity. They underscore emigration and immigration as selective processes involving some people and not others. One implication is that immigrants possess a strong work ethic and high aspirations to improve themselves. These are traits that lend themselves to economic and social integration, even amid the difficulties of resettling in a new society.

In thinking about international migration as a selective process, consider the fact that although immigrants number in the many millions, they have not constituted a significant percentage of any society they left. For example, few nations sent as many people abroad as Norway, from which 677,000 emigrated between 1865 and 1915, mostly to America. In the 1860s, Norwegians emigrants numbering 40 percent of the recent increase in the population of Norway lived outside that country for lack of faith they could survive there. Based on gradual improvements in living standards, even as the population continued to increase, over time the number of emigrants declined. By the 1890s, although 20 percent of those of Norwegian birth lived outside Norway, most Norwegians stayed at home. During the great age of European emigration, the same could be said of Europe in general: only three persons per thousand emigrated, and some countries, such as France and the Netherlands, sent many fewer people abroad than others. In 2015, while just over a quarter billion people throughout the world resided outside the country of their birth, they were no more than 3 percent of the world's population.

Within all countries of emigration, particularized local, regional, occupational, and communal streams have differentiated these relatively few individuals on the move from the vast majority who chose not to migrate. Attempting to know emigrants by nation alone may limit our understanding. While what is attention-grabbing about people in terms of their history, language, culture, and appearance seems most easily explained by nationality, this is not necessarily the best way to understand international population movements.

Moreover, international migrants have sought multiple destinations, not just the United States. Many moved first within their own countries, from rural areas to towns and cities. They moved to nearby countries seasonally or permanently, as did Poles migrating to France and Germany and Italians migrating to France, Germany, and Switzerland to work in agriculture, mining, and factories. Chinese have for centuries migrated in search of work and trade throughout Southeast Asia. Japanese began to migrate as contract laborers to work on Hawaiian plantations before Hawaii became an American colony in 1898. So many became permanent residents of the islands that, by 1940, there were twice as many Japanese residents of Hawaii as there were living on the American mainland. During these same decades the Japanese were also establishing themselves, as were the Chinese, in significant numbers in Brazil and Peru, where they provided much-needed wage labor as well as commercial services in societies with a small middle class. A century ago, Australia, Argentina, Brazil, Chile, Canada, and South Africa were attracting a wide variety of peoples from many of the same points of origin as the United States. By the late twentieth century, almost every developed or rapidly developing society, whether in North or South America, western Europe, West Africa, the Gulf States, or

Australia and New Zealand, attracted immigrants from poorer or less developed countries.

Immigration has not necessarily been a permanent condition for all those who leave their homelands, and this, too, helps in understanding its selectivity and purposefulness as a process. As part of a long-range plan, or because of unemployment, homesickness, physical illness, or a failure to realize their goals, immigrants have often chosen to re-emigrate. From 1908 to 1923, a period that saw the highest incidence of European immigration to the United States, approximately 3 to 3.5 million people re-emigrated. To make the picture more complex, some of these individuals eventually chose to return to the United States, though how many and for how long is unknown.

Movement across oceans and the transnational planning it required were facilitated by advancements in transportation. During the age of sailing craft, the unpleasant, unhealthy voyage of approximately four to six weeks across the Atlantic from Europe was an experience few wanted to repeat, though some certainly did. Seasickness and fever diseases afflicted even the heartiest individuals, and burials at sea formed traumatic memories. The great steamships significantly reduced the cost (at least for the cheapest ticket), danger, discomfort, and duration (to a week to ten days) of the journey and, like jet aircraft for today's migrants, made it possible to travel with much greater facility. Increasingly, the shipping lines formed agreements with the railroads that allowed individuals to be ticketed through, with guidance offered, to inland destinations. As construction workers, building artisans, and skilled textile workers began to integrate job markets in their homelands and in the United States, seasonal, transoceanic commuting relationships became possible for those who could afford it. In a world of air travel, such possibilities seem easier than ever. But most immigrants have limited means. Such is the case with contemporary immigrants to the United States from the Caribbean. Transportation to their homelands is easily found, but every dollar spent on travel is a dollar less to support more costly lives in America or to send to their island families.

The immigrants discussed in the next two chapters are not confused, rootless people who are hostages to forces beyond their control. Men and women, farmers and industrial workers, shop owners and domestic workers, adults and children—they are all less violently uprooted from familiar circumstances than they are self-transplanted into more promising settings. The historian John Bodnar has suggested the mentality that has typified such modern immigrants is pragmatic. Open to change, they test the world to see what works in responding to it and then adopt strategies to succeed, while acknowledging the need to continue to readjust amid constant change.

This flexible, risk-taking modern mentality has been placed mostly in defense of traditional and conservative goals—security and stability, especially for family, measured in terms of improvements in housing, diet, and clothing rather than in wealth and extravagant consumption. The typical immigrant's mentality may also be said to be that of a venturesome conservative, employing new strategies in pursuit of recognizably traditional aspirations. Immigration and resettlement have their tragic dimensions; leaving one's homeland, familiar circumstances, and friends and family is never easy. Immigrants have often been poor in the places of resettlement, and they have done backbreaking and dangerous work. But theirs is also a story of creativity in prevailing over difficulty and of small but real gains that have increased security, prosperity, and dignity on their own terms.

Chapter 4

Mass population movements and resettlement, 1820–1924

Large-scale, transformative social processes framed boundaries within which mass international migration out of Europe occurred after 1820. Within a century, the historical purpose of international migration was realized: societies with too many people exported their surplus population to emergent societies needing labor in the Western Hemisphere and Australasia. These receiving societies were principally the United States (35 million), Argentina (6 million), Canada (5 million), Brazil (4 million), and Australia (3.5 million), all rich in resources, especially arable land, but lacking population sufficient to develop them. In 1800 only 4 percent of Europeans were living outside Europe and Russian Siberia; in 1914, by which time about 60 million people over a century had left Europe, approximately 21 percent of Europeans were living outside the continent. The population of the United States would have been only 60 percent of the numbers achieved by 1940 without international migration. That additional 40 percent made vital contributions to the country becoming the world's largest economy.

Colonialism also spread Europeans throughout the world. Some colonial powers used settler colonies, such as Algeria or Indonesia, to create opportunities for hundreds of thousands, while also extending national power. Thus, colonial migrations might supplant voluntary immigration to other sovereign states as a way of dealing with excess population. Possessing the largest empire in the world in the nineteenth century, Great Britain sent millions of military personnel, civil servants, colonial officials, and settlers to far-flung colonial destinations. Nonetheless, it had the third-largest number of immigrants (4,782,000) in the United States, after Germany and Italy, between 1820 and 1970. For continental Europe as a whole, nothing matched international voluntary emigration as a way of shedding people.

A fateful demographic transition that began in Europe and would reach the rest of the world during the twentieth century has been at the heart of the rise of modern immigration. After 1750 Europe's population began a very rapid ascent, first in western Europe and then, by the mid-nineteenth century, in central, southern, and eastern Europe. Much of this growth is explained by improvements in diet that were made possible, for example, by the cultivation of the potato, originally a New World crop. The potato was a principal staple of peasant diets until catastrophic crop failures occurred due to a fungus in the 1840s in France, the Netherlands, some of the German states, the Scottish Highlands, and especially Ireland, where a million people died of starvation and disease and 1.7 million were forced to emigrate. In addition, long before the mid-twentieth-century antibiotic revolution, improvements in sanitation, including more potable drinking water, better waste disposal, and aseptic child-birthing, brought down mortality rates.

Typically, there was no significant expansion in the amount of arable land, so population growth placed pressure on food supplies for the peasant majority, which was engaged in a wide variety of land-owning, leasing, or renting relationships characteristic of European agriculture. Even land of no more than marginal value was for sale at escalating prices. Leaving the land often seemed the only way to survive. That was only one facet of the crisis in agriculture. The growth of population and related rise of people living in the industrial cities encouraged the commercialization of agriculture, through which the cultivation of both food and fiber, using technology and scientific cultivation, was placed on an industrial footing. Peasants were reduced to wage laborers in rural areas, and their customary rights, including long-term lease arrangements, were destroyed.

Key to the process of commercialization was the consolidation of small holdings. Extensive cultivation over vast acreage created the basis for significant economies of scale and a vast potential for production and profit. Landlords were quick to realize that the traditional patchwork pattern of small holdings farmed by people who were often only barely surviving, and the common lands they shared for grazing work animals and livestock, were antithetical to capitalist agriculture. Consolidation might be accomplished by increasing rents, outright evictions, or simply declaring that, after the deaths of the current renters, the property would be unavailable for leasing. Thus, peasants lost their access to the long-term arrangements that provided security, and they might then be reduced to urban or rural wage labor.

Some large economies outside Europe experienced similar developments in the mid- and late nineteenth century. In the late 1860s Japan began a wholesale program of industrialization and urban development that encouraged wealthy landowners to consolidate holdings and, hence, to remove the peasantry. In southeastern China change was initiated from without, as the European economic penetration of the densely populated valley and delta of the Pearl River placed pressures on the peasant population. In central Mexico, change came rapidly to the heartland of peasant agriculture after the completion of railroad lines north to the border cities in the 1890s. In anticipation of the opening of the American and Mexican urban markets to indigenous agriculture, Mexican landlords began agglomerating peasant holdings and created great estates of as many as 40,000 acres. Some of these large landowners were content to sell off their increasingly valuable holdings, but while the peasantry went landless, the government of President Porfirio Díaz sought out European commercial farmers to buy these lands, believing that they would achieve greater crop yields, and thus a heartier commercial agriculture, than the subsistence-oriented peasantry.

The response of peasants to the collapse of accustomed ways of rural life was complex. They might assume traditional forms of resistance, such as riots, arson, and the killing of the commercial herds displacing them. Or it might take modern forms, such as rent strikes and lawsuits orchestrated by well-organized tenants' unions. But political protest was a difficult route, because peasants were opposed by powerful modernizing social classes that controlled state power, or were allied with those who did, and often used it in the most brutal, insidious ways.

More common were nonpolitical, individualized strategies undertaken within the framework of the family. The traditional family, with its patriarchal authority, maternal domestic organization, and insistence on children's economic contributions, might be effectively mobilized for mutual support. Younger children might be sent off to become laborers and servants. Marriage might be postponed, as in Japan and Ireland, to shorten the period of the young couple's independence, simultaneously lowering births by truncating the years of marital fertility. Family forms might be changed, too. In the European countryside, more complicated family arrangements—for example, stem families in which one son and his family might live with his parents, or joint families, in which all sons and their families lived with parents—arose for the purpose of increasing labor power, living cheaply in a common household, and meeting the challenge of higher rents.

Another option was migration, whether long- or short-distance. A high degree of transiency, especially among the young, came to characterize the peasantry. In many places, transiency had been a routine feature of the peasant economy for centuries. Younger men in particular traveled to get work helping with harvests. But, as modernizing transformations gathered force, many more people engaged in short-distance migrations, which became less about supplementing income and more about survival. Seasonal transiency might expand to encompass a larger portion of the year. Nearby migrations in search of work as laborers in the new proletarianized, commercial agriculture grew common.

Exerting a more powerful pull was the vast labor market of the industrial economy in the growing cities, where technology and entrepreneurship had merged, first in textiles, to create mass production on a scale previously unimaginable. The new factory system, with its low-priced goods, simultaneously undercut the competitive position of village and town artisans and craftsmen, whose livelihoods were already imperiled by the problems that plagued their traditional market, the peasantry. In consequence, traditionally skilled artisans joined the growing stream of migrants to cities.

It was bad enough, from his perspective, for the shoemaker to tend a machine in a shoe factory. For many peasants, a permanent descent into wage earning could only be confronted with horror. They measured value by the possession of land, whether as owners or renters, and strove to be as independent as possible in achieving their means of survival. For both peasants and traditional craftsmen to end up living the proletarian life of a wage earner in the slums of nearby industrial cities was a miserable fate. Many millions did suffer that fate, however; indeed, without them, there would have been no Industrial Revolution in Europe. Although it is difficult to know the numbers involved, rural and village folk who came to regional industrial centers might well have been engaged in step-migrations, ultimately using the wages made in factory work to finance international migration.

International migration was a strategy for avoiding proletarianization and might fill multiple practical needs, including permanent resettlement, temporary work abroad while earning money to be brought back to the homeland to ensure stability in the new economy, and earning money to provide remittances sent to family at home. The volume of these remittances sent from the United States was impressive. Between 1870 and 1914, in the currency values of the day, for example, Slovaks sent approximately $200 million home; between 1897 and 1902, Italians sent $100 million; and between 1906 and 1930, Swedes sent $192 million. Greek remittances grew annually between 1910 and 1920 from $4.675 million to $110 million.

International migration was best considered not by the very poor, for whom it was prohibitively expensive, but by the middle and lower-middle ranks of rural, village, and town society. They possessed the material resources to emigrate, such as fare for ships' passage and funds to aid in resettlement, but also the nonmaterial cultural capital, chief among which was literacy. This is not to say the very poor were always absent from the ranks of emigrants. Though not the poorest of their singularly immiserated society, the approximately 1.7 million Potato Famine Irish migrants of the 1840s and 1850s were uniquely impoverished as a cohort among immigrants to the United States. As the price of the cheapest passage declined with the coming of steamships, it became easier for poorer people to emigrate.

Understanding the consequences of poverty must be further contextualized in the later emigration epoch. In contrast to the resettlement of the Potato Famine Irish, who were the first generation of mass Irish Catholic emigration, by the later nineteenth century many of the poorer immigrants were members of transnational support networks that bound them to family, kin, and friends already in the United States. Practical support, which might include small sums of money as well as lodging and a prearranged job, often compensated for lack of funds on arrival.

In the nineteenth century, when cheap, accessible land was plentiful, immigrants could dream of replicating an old way of life in the newly emerging states of the Midwest and Great Plains, where the flat prairie lands were known for remarkable fertility. Husbands and wives, with young children, in search of farmsteads were especially prominent among mid-nineteenth-century Germans and Scandinavians. There were single male migrants, too, both farmers and artisans, who hoped to stay for a year or two and make enough money to return to Europe to start families and to buy and farm their own land. They might work in mills, factories, or mines, even if they would not take such work in Europe. American wages were higher, and there was less reason to fear the trap of proletarianization if one had the means for returning home with the money to support a farm. Others worked in American mills in the hope of raising the capital to start American farms and achieve independence from the wage economy.

Skilled workers in infant American industries, such as beer- and wine-making, pottery, textiles, and stone quarrying, were also found among the nineteenth-century immigrants, especially those from Great Britain. Capitalists could not yet find sufficient numbers of Americans with the knowledge to operate industrial technologies that had emerged first in Europe. In the pioneering phase of a number of industries, the importation of skilled Europeans, lured by high wages, was essential to achieving progress. Such migrations were targeted geographically and, if continued over time, might lead to a virtual international integration of local labor forces, such as took place over many years among skilled stonecutters between the sandstone quarries of Yorkshire's southern Pennine fringe and those of northwestern New York State.

The changing character of European immigration

The decline after 1890 in the reserves of arable American land that could be conveniently traveled to from the principal East Coast immigrant-receiving ports, the subsequent rise in the price of farmlands, and the growth of mass production industries altered the character of immigration. The demographic balance of international migration increasingly shifted from young families to single men in search of urban employment. A significant percentage of them aspired to work as long as necessary to make enough money to return to their homelands and achieve a greater measure of independence there. Men predominated two to one over women, except among the Irish. In the international migrations of the nineteenth and early twentieth centuries, women were mostly wives, mothers, and daughters arriving in family groups, but the situation was different among the Irish. In Ireland women had few opportunities. Marriage was being postponed later and later, or had become impossible, as available farmland declined. Irish women did well in American job markets, especially as domestics, because they spoke English. By the 1870s, only some 15 percent of the Irish emigration was composed of families. Irish men and women were just about equal in immigration streams to the United States between 1870 and 1920, although women outnumbered men in approximately half of those years.

The decades after 1890 were peak years for the European "birds of passage"—male transients who took advantage of transoceanic steamships to commute between their homelands and the United States. Italians were among the most transient immigrant peoples. Italian construction and agricultural laborers and railroad track maintenance workers moved routinely in search of employment in their lines of work between the United States, Argentina, or Brazil and their homelands. Among British workers, building artisans regularly worked both sides of the Atlantic. These immigrant workers integrated the labor markets on both sides of the Atlantic.

The birds of passage must be distinguished from those noncommuting migrants who arrived with the intention of making money and then leaving to fulfill aspirations in their homelands. Perhaps a quarter of those entering the United States re-emigrated. From 1908 to 1923, approximately 89 percent of Bulgarians, Serbians, and Montenegrins, 66 percent of Romanians and Hungarians, and 60 percent of southern Italians returned to Europe. Among peoples who had little to return to because of a lack of opportunities, such as the Irish (11 percent) or, because of persecution, the eastern European Jews (5 percent), re-emigrants were far fewer.

Seventy-five percent stayed in the United States. Some men had always planned to send for their families, if they could find a promising situation. Others gradually came to the conclusion that they would be better off breaking with the past. Though a minority, Europeans who re-emigrated had a strong influence on the discourse of immigration restrictionists. They sent money home rather than spend it to the benefit of American commerce. They had no desire to assimilate. The labor unions saw them as willing tools of the employers, impossible to organize.

A different picture emerged on the Pacific Coast. In these more recently settled states, arable land was still available. Young Japanese immigrant families sought farmland in rural California, Washington, and Oregon. Young South Asian men from the Punjab came to the Imperial Valley of California, where large fruit and vegetable farms were being carved out of the desert alongside massive irrigation projects, to work as agricultural laborers. Many hoped to earn the money to buy small farms and form families, as some did with Mexican women, starting a unique Punjabi–Mexican hybrid ethnicity. In contrast, Mexicans displaced by landlords first became a local agrarian proletariat or went to work in factories and mines in northern Mexico, where wages were higher than in agriculture. Spurred by the promise of even higher wages and eventually threatened by revolutionary violence, after

1900 they began entering the United States in growing numbers to find work in mining and agriculture in the American West.

To casual observers, mass immigration may seem chaotic and even menacingly disorderly. But this is less often the perception of immigrants, whose strategies for accomplishing relocation have been heavily dependent on paths laid down by those often familiar individuals who came before them. Every immigration has its pioneers with compelling narratives of exploration and discovery. Once these pioneers lay down tracks, even the most massive immigrant flow takes on a predictable character. That is the mark of the immigrant's creativity in living: in the midst of life-changing movements across vast distances, they have been guided by strategies that minimize risks and extend the realm of the familiar. People hoping to improve themselves by pursuing work across international space have always been a selective group. Hard work, high aspirations, and family and group solidarity are characteristic of immigrating groups and provide substantial resources in the effort to make new homes.

Chapter 5

Mass population movements and resettlement, 1965 to the present

By the 1970s, when the memory of the complex pasts of the immigrants of the late nineteenth and early twentieth centuries were fading and they had largely achieved social and political integration, the United States was experiencing a massive immigration wave. It was made possible by the 1965 changes in immigration law and facilitated by the loosening grip both of colonialism throughout the non-European world and of authoritarian regimes, such as the Soviet Union, the People's Republic of China, and small states such as Haiti and the Dominican Republic. In 2014–15, the United States was the world's largest recipient of international migrants, receiving 3,130,000 people, fully one in five of the world's migrants. The nation had a total of some 42 million foreign-born residents. (Germany, the second-ranking recipient, had some 12 million foreign-born residents.) This was about 13.3 percent of the total American population, considerably below 22 percent in Canada, with a tenth of America's people, qualifying somewhat the claim that the country was being overwhelmed by immigration. Nonetheless, it represents a vast increase over 1960, when, amid low immigration totals, there were 9.7 million foreign-born residents, or 5.4 percent of the population. This percentage was almost exactly the same as in 1910, when the percentage of foreign-born had reached its then all-time high.

How has this massive immigration compared to the previous great migrations? While there certainly have been profound changes in the world since the earlier international migration waves, the underlying reasons for people to voluntarily leave their homelands have not changed greatly. Much in the nature of the current of international movement today is a variation on older themes enhanced by new technologies.

Contemporary migration is the consequence of the spreading out of modernizing processes to the developing societies of Asia, Africa, and Latin America. Population growth occasioned by decreasing mortality due to better nutrition, sanitation, and medical care, combined with the commercialization of agriculture, urbanization, and industrialization, have produced a surplus of labor in societies that cannot guarantee even educated, credentialed individuals adequate living standards, or ones comparable to more advanced societies. However, political instability and war, as in Southeast Asia from the 1950s through the 1970s, Central America in the 1980s, West Africa in the 1990s, and Libya, Syria, and Central and East Africa in the new century, have now added significantly to socioeconomic dislocations, creating massive refugee flows. Rapidly evolving electronic media play the same role in disseminating knowledge of faraway alternatives that print media, personal correspondence, and the telegraph once played and provide new resources for maintaining immigrant networks and migration chains. Jet transportation now speeds contemporary international migrants to their destinations.

While there are many international destinations for contemporary international migrants, three factors have made the United States attractive. First, there is geographic proximity, which makes immigration relatively cheap even for the poorer citizens of Mexico and the developing, poorer nations of Central and South America and the Caribbean. In 2015 approximately 23.2 million of the foreign-born in the United States (nearly 50 percent of the foreign-born total) were from Western Hemisphere, with

11.6 million from Mexico alone. (South and East Asia were next in continental rank order, at 12 million.) Second, after 1965, American immigration laws, alongside those of Canada and Australia, have been especially welcoming, even as the visa process became backlogged due to heightened security after 9/11. The family reconstitution priority of American law, continuing to take precedence over skills, facilitates the work of creating migration chains. Third, American media and consumer goods have penetrated the world beyond Europe, globalizing visions of the American way of life. Noteworthy, of course, is the rapidity with which knowledge spreads across the world, the astounding volume of information transmitted, and the speed and convenience with which international immigrants reach their destinations.

While the scale of global immigration is impressive, migration remains a selective process. Most people continue to reside in the countries of their birth, and if they must relocate to seek opportunity, they fulfill that need through short-distance migrations within their homelands. In 2005, when they were the leading exporters of people to America, Mexico and China, with emigrant populations of 797,000 and 380,000, respectively, were also in the midst of explosions of urban populations, as people in both countries left the countryside, where they could no longer survive on small farms or on farm wage labor. Mexico City, Monterrey, Shanghai, Beijing, and other Mexican and Chinese cities have experienced explosive growth.

The impact of contemporary immigration on the United States

The face of the United States is now being remade as dramatically as it was by the previous mass immigration waves. There has been a nationalization of immigration, because dispersal of ethnic and racial diversity has occurred on a scale previously unknown. Sections of the country that experienced little international migration in the past, principally the American South, are taking in large numbers of immigrants. This is a consequence of the shift in industrial activity after 1960 from the high-wage, unionized localities of northern and midwestern states to the low-wage, non–labor union southern states, which greatly expanded the southern economy.

The South, which historically had a vast reserve of low-wage labor in its African American population, did not experience much European immigrant settlement, and it never had significant numbers of Hispanics. Although most Mexican migrants continue to reside in the West and Southwest, for the first time such southern states as North Carolina, Georgia, and Arkansas have large Mexican minorities. Meanwhile, other regions, such as the Upper Midwest and the Great Plains, which had not experienced immigrant settlement since the nineteenth century, have experienced immigration again. While racial diversity was a constant throughout southern history, towns in such states as Kansas, Iowa, and Minnesota, experiencing the settlement of Mexicans, Somalis, Ethiopian, and Sudanese meatpacking and chicken-processing workers, had never experienced broad-scale, international racial diversity.

The sociologist Nancy Foner has demonstrated how the two great immigration gateways, New York City and Los Angeles, serve as dramatic examples of immigration creating singular, localized patterns of diversity. New York City continues its long history of racial and ethnic diversity. As in the past, its mixture of peoples is as broad as their numbers are large. In 1920, 36 percent of its population (or 2 million people) was composed of immigrants; in 2016, the figure was an exactly comparable 37 percent (3.2 million). New York is singular both in that it has continued to receive some of the same European immigrants, principally Poles and residents of the former Soviet Union, and that its communities of newer, non-European immigrants in some cases build on existing populations. Its populations of foreign-born people of color originally date from a century ago, when Caribbean islanders established themselves. Jamaicans, Grenadians, Haitians, and others are now joined by Africans from Senegal, Nigeria, Ghana, and elsewhere in sub-Saharan Africa. Since the 1940s, New York City has had a sizeable enough Puerto Rican population that Spanish is often heard on the streets. That population has been joined by large numbers of Hispanic peoples from throughout the Caribbean and South and Central America. The city had the largest Chinese population outside California in the twentieth century, and the Asian population has become vastly more diverse, with substantial Korean, Southeast Asian, and Philippine immigrations.

California has had Mexican and Asian populations since it became part of the United States, but their tentative legal status long placed limits on growth. Since 1980 the Los Angeles metropolitan area has been a magnet for contemporary immigration. It manifests different patterns than New York City. Like such southwestern cities as Houston, Phoenix, and Tucson, with proximity to the Mexican border, Los Angeles attracts both legal and illegal Mexican migrants. Moreover, its relative proximity to Asia has made it attractive to transpacific migration. In addition to becoming a destination for the same Asian peoples who have settled in New York, Los Angeles is home to America's largest concentrations of Cambodians, Laotians, and Vietnamese. A number of suburban cities and towns in the Los Angeles and San Francisco metropolitan areas have Asian majorities or near-majorities.

Significant demographic transformations are also observed in the displacement of African Americans by Hispanics as the nation's largest minority group in major American cities. Radical shifts in population ratios are taking place between African Americans and Hispanics, leading to dramatic changes in local electoral power and cultural authority. In 1960 blacks were 20 percent and Hispanics 5 percent of the population of Houston, whereas in

2018 they represented 23 percent and 44 percent, respectively. In 1970 blacks were 17 percent of Los Angeles's population, but they were only 9 percent of the city's population in 2018, while in the same three decades, Hispanics had grown from 18 percent to 48 percent. In Miami, where the Cuban population of immigrants and refugees has grown enormously since the 1959 revolution, Cubans have become the largest ethnic group, to be joined in later decades by refugees and voluntary immigrants from Central and South America. The percentage of Hispanics in Miami's population almost tripled between 1970 and 2020, reaching 70 percent in 2019, while that of African Americans increased from 15 percent to 19 percent. Where Hispanics have yet to overtake African Americans, they seem likely to do so in the near future. Chicago had the third largest Hispanic population, with 778,800 (28 percent), very largely Mexican and settled there since 1970. African Americans numbered 887,600 in the city in 2019. Hispanics were the fastest-growing segment of Chicago's population during this period. In the 1990s, though black (37 percent) and non-Hispanic white (32 percent) population growth had recently been falling because of suburbanization and declining birth rates, only the number of Hispanics actually rose in Chicago. In total, by 2019, while African Americans were about 13.4 percent (44 million) of the American population, Hispanics had approached 18.3 percent (61 million).

As the example of New York City suggests, the peoples who make up the post-1965 migration are not all strangers to America. The networks and chains that have been instrumental in forming these populations sometimes date from pre-1965 voluntary migrations. They were facilitated by national ties developed under circumstances of American colonialism; exemptions of individual countries in the Western Hemisphere from the 1924 quota legislation; and small-scale, voluntary international migration streams, such as among the Chinese. While the early Cold War facilitated the acceptance as refugees and immigrants of American allies among Taiwan Chinese, Koreans, and Southeast Asian refugees and immigrants, it disrupted ties with Mainland China, Laos, Vietnam, and Cambodia. Not until changes in bilateral relations took place between the 1970s and 2000 did those Asian peoples immigrate to the United States in significant numbers.

The structure of contemporary immigration

International voluntary migrations continue to be constructed less along the lines of nations than those of social classes, gender, regions and localities, and occupations. Within these migration streams, networks and chain migrations based on family and communal relations are still the ultimate determinant of which individuals emigrate and where they resettle. The 1965 immigration law gave greater significance to the network by giving family reunification the highest priority in granting visas.

How these networks and chains form and function for contemporary international migrants is seen in microcosm in the Boston area. The sociologist Peggy Leavitt has demonstrated translocal connections between Mira Flores, a small village in the south of the Dominican Republic, and the Boston area, where 71,000 Dominicans lived in 2016. Here Dominicans have been seeking work for decades in small factories and service businesses. Using savings, some opened small stores that tap the Dominican market. In 1994, more than 65 percent of the 545 households in Mira Flores had relatives in the Boston area, and 60 percent of those households reported receiving monthly remittances from relatives in the United States. The difficulties of living in Mira Flores are evident in that, for 40 percent of those receiving remittances, this money was between 75 and 100 percent of total household income. Similar localized connections and dependencies exist between the massive Dominican population of Washington Heights in New York City and people in other Dominican towns and villages. In 1995, $796 million in remittances were sent to that Caribbean nation from the United States. By 2017, the 1.1 million Dominican migrants were sending

$6 billion in remittances to their island homeland. Those who re-emigrated with money earned in the United States were a substantial spur to the Dominican economy, spending their American savings on houses, household goods, automobiles, and homes.

In social and economic terms, most contemporary international migrants continue to come from the middle rungs of society. They are farm owners, skilled workers, shopkeepers, teachers, accountants, office managers, building contractors, and small manufacturers. They cannot attain incomes in their homelands that allow them to buy homes and household appliances and modern plumbing, to which they have been exposed by global media. Today's migration streams do depart from past immigrants, who were generally not educated beyond elementary literacy skills—and need not have been in light of the requirements (a strong back and the ability to tend a machine) of industrializing economies. Contemporary American job markets are different than in the past, because of the movement toward a mixed (service, healthcare, electronic technology, and manufacturing) economy. Newer immigrants are often educated and technically trained individuals, such as credentialed Asian information technology workers. In spite of decades of high growth and excellent public educational systems, the economies of countries such as India, Korea, and Taiwan have failed to create sufficient well-paying employment to absorb all their educated younger workers, who are often forced to take low-paying jobs or consider emigration.

With its concern for creating foundations for continuing economic development, American policy has deepened this brain drain from the developing world. The old ban on contract labor has been relaxed for skilled technical and health-related professional workers, such as nurses. If these individuals can prove that they come with prearranged jobs, the visa process is expedited. In the search for such white-collar work, English-speaking migrants from South Asia, the Philippines, and the former British Caribbean have an advantage. Travel agencies and private labor recruitment agencies work together to facilitate the admission of these migrants. Moreover, the H-1B visa program, which created a special track for a broad array of educated technical and specialized workers, offers renewable visas of between six and ten years' duration. The holder of one of these visas has an expedited path to permanent residence, obtaining a "green card," as many H-1B entrants have done.

As this migration stream suggests, though popular images of contemporary immigrants are of blue-collar workers, the occupational profile is more complex than ever before. A 2010 survey found that largely because of American policy combined with the greater educational and skill base or the possession on arrival of some capital, the 25 million legal immigrants in the United States who lived in the largest metropolitan areas—nearly two-thirds of all immigrants—were almost evenly distributed across wide bands of occupations and incomes. In fourteen of the twenty-five largest metropolitan areas, between 51 and 80 percent of the immigrants have been found in white-collar employment, including business ownership, the sciences, healthcare, and electronic technology. In these metropolitan areas, the percentage of white-collar workers among immigrants was never smaller than a third of the total of immigrants employed.

Blue-collar work continues to be common among immigrants. Agriculture, construction, and building maintenance work play a larger role in immigrant employment—and slightly more so, as 2017 data revealed, for illegal immigrants than for legal ones. Today's immigrants do not have access to as broad a range of stable, relatively high-paying blue-collar jobs in mass production industries as in the past. Yet there is still employment in mass production industries and in traditional factory-type settings. Jobs are sometimes found in fields in which immigrant labor traditionally worked and where immigrants again have formed ethnic niches providing relatively reliable, if not necessarily well-paid, safe, or sanitary, employment. Just as a century ago the packing houses of the great Chicago stockyards depended on thousands of eastern European Poles, Lithuanians, Jews, and Bohemians, today Mexicans, Somalis, Ethiopians, and others find work in meatpacking and chicken-processing plants. As in the past, immigrants were routed to these locations initially by recruiters and then by people from their homeland communities or families who arrived before them. Faced with international competition and subject to a relentless process of consolidation under international corporations, these plants have seen a radical compression of wages, favoring low-cost immigrant labor. Wages at a major meatpacking plant in Oelwein, Iowa, which has widely employed immigrants, fell within a few years from $18 an hour to just over $6, then doubled by 2020, while still remaining several dollars below the earlier figure.

Another example is provided by the garment industry, which has suffered intense competitive international pressure. Just as eastern European Jews and some Italians once found a niche there, whether as workers or subcontractors for larger firms, in the much reduced, present-day American garment industry, Chinese immigrants in New York City and Los Angeles are now employed as both workers in sweatshop-like settings reminiscent of the past and as subcontractors. In 2014, 22 percent of legal immigrants and an estimated 14 percent of illegal ones were found working in clothing and textiles.

Not all contemporary ethnic niches are in industry. Chinese and Southeast Asians own small restaurants and take-out fast-food shops and perform culinary work, while Koreans operate as green-grocers in New York City and Los Angeles. With personal savings or loans from relatives, Koreans sometimes come to America with the intention of opening a small store. They enhance their chances of surviving an unpredictable market by utilizing unpaid family labor, as do Chinese in the prepared food business. Grandparents are enlisted into the work force, often to watch small children, while older siblings and parents work in the family enterprise. As in the past, the ethnic market for goods and services, offered in the language of the homeland, also remains a source of opportunity for small retailers, especially in cities like Miami, Los Angeles, and New York, where immigrants form immense consumer markets. But immigrants in big cities are just as engaged in carving out niches for themselves in small food or retailing businesses that serve the general American market for goods and services.

This profile of the diversity of contemporary immigrant occupations suggests that, even in the uncertain economy of the early twenty-first century, many immigrants have found a place for themselves or are hopeful of doing so. However, millions of immigrants are not in the country legally. While their lives are harder to track because of their status, it is clear they do not have the same prospects as legal residents. Illegal status limits prosperity and security. These immigrants lead a shadow existence, and they risk losing not only their jobs, but also any property they have come to own if they are discovered and deported to their homelands.

The numerical predominance of women

That contemporary immigrant occupational streams, such as healthcare and sewing in garment shops, contain large numbers of adult women, especially single women, contrasts with the past. Though the extent of female numerical predominance varies greatly by group and within different areas of the United States, women have made up the majority of immigrants of a number of Asian, Central and South American, and Caribbean island groups for much of the period of the recent immigration. In 2015, nationally, women made up 51.4 percent of voluntary immigrants to the United States, and men were 48.6 percent. In New York City by the early 1990s, sex ratios varied to the extent that women had a slight numerical advantage among Chinese and Dominicans and made up as much as two-thirds of Colombian and Philippine immigrants.

A century ago, immigrant women stayed at home and their children left school to work, but today the pattern has been reversing. In New York City in 1990, 60 percent of immigrant women aged sixteen to sixty-five were wage earning, and among Filipinas, Jamaicans, Trinidadians, Haitians, and Guyanese—all groups profiting in the search for employment as English speakers—seven in ten or more were employed. In 2015 immigrant women made up about 28 percent (2.8 million) of the city's wage earners. They work at all levels of employment, from highly paid professions to low-wage manufacturing and domestic and personal service.

Women's predominance in contemporary migration streams is a result of changes in law and economic restructuring in the last third of the twentieth century. Opportunity has become more concentrated in light manufacturing, domestic and personal service, and healthcare. These are traditionally women's fields, because of female traditions of caregiving and housekeeping, and of gendered employer assumptions that women are more likely to accept dead-end, low-wage, and monotonous detail work.

Such assumptions about women's work, however, do not automatically translate into low-wage work. It is true that immigrant men and women are often overqualified for the work they have to take. Technical training and higher education in one's homeland do not lead to equivalent employment if one lacks English-language proficiency or the ability to meet American licensing and professional standards. But when training or education has been shaped to international standards in the developed world, immigrants possessing English have often gotten work commensurate with their level of preparation.

96

An example comes from the Philippines. Because of fear of political unrest caused by unemployment, especially among educated young people, the Philippine government after 1974 geared state and private agencies to facilitating emigration. The government was also eager to see remittance income returned to the country to spur economic development and relieve poverty. A significant aspect of this strategy has been investment in quality nursing education to prepare women for positions abroad, so they are now found in relatively high-paying healthcare work in the United States. In the late twentieth century, trained nurses from the English-speaking islands of the Caribbean also found extensive employment in US hospitals and eldercare facilities, especially in eastern states. In 2020, when their work was highlighted by the frontline roles they played in the coronavirus pandemic, immigrant women, the majority English-speaking Asian (many of them Filipina) and Caribbean migrants, constituted fully 74 percent of all New York City healthcare workers. Immigrant women also made up 51 percent of those nonprofessionals employed in child care and eldercare in the city.

In light of the availability of such work, women have found it easier to obtain labor certifications that attest to the fact that they will be employed, and therefore to receive a visa. Consequently, in another sharp historical contrast, women have often been the pioneers in forging migration networks and chains, establishing themselves and then using family reunification programs to resettle their children and husbands. Husbands frequently lose status relative to their dominant position in the homeland. Their dependence on their wives is deepened when they are more often unemployed than women or paid less when working.

Under these circumstances, men have reluctantly become housekeepers and caregivers to children, which offends their sense of the proper order of gender relations and may result in depression, nostalgia, and a desire to re-emigrate. Even though working immigrant women often continue nonetheless to perform traditional household duties, many of them are less enthusiastic about surrendering the relative independence that comes with earning their own living and with American social and cultural support for gender equity. If they were to return to their homelands, they might be expected to leave the labor market and resume traditional roles. Some women, however, regard re-emigration positively, as a key to not having to work, even if it is accompanied by the return of their husbands' traditional authority. The old role of housewife becomes acceptable if savings from American wages enable a better living standard in a new home, with an American-style kitchen and modern appliances and plumbing.

Nonetheless, there are many stories of women and men who were nurses, teachers, dentists, or office workers in their homelands who, for want of adequate credentials and out of economic necessity, become trapped cleaning homes and offices or doing unskilled attendant care or food service work in hospitals. They are too poor to return home and live with enhanced if meager prosperity, but their American lives are insecure and prosperity continues to elude them.

In the recent past, with all of the insecurity in American job markets, which exacerbates the risk-taking inherent in immigration, it is logical to ask what immigrants gain, especially those who commit themselves to staying permanently. A century ago many newcomers could at least count on some evidence of rapid improvement, if only relative to the miserable circumstances they had left. In confronting the paradox of choosing downward mobility, it is necessary to remember the strategizing, pragmatic mentality characterizing international migrants. Immigration is judged a better long-term solution to the problem of achieving an acceptable, secure standard of living than remaining at home. While the immigrant generation might experience disappointment, parents convince themselves that their children will live better than they do. They sustain these hopes even as they worry about young people's exposure in America to drugs, gangs, violence, sexual license, and antisocial attitudes challenging the authority of clergy, parents, teachers, and police. Immigration remains a gamble, and resettlement is a tentative process that demands the energy and intelligence of those who choose to give up their old homes to improve themselves in new ones.

Part III

The dialogue of ethnicity and assimilation

Throughout American history, there has been anxiety over a perceived unwillingness of immigrants to become Americans. The public expressions of this concern are similar from one era to another, even as the origins and circumstances of the immigrants might change. They have depended, first, on the assumption that the immigrant's ethnicity is evidence of resistance to integration to American society, rather than of a desire for a supportive communal affiliation and sustaining identity amid the challenges of emigration and resettlement. Second, they proceed on the doubtful essentialist premise that there is an unchanging core American culture and identity, descended directly from colonial British stock and the Founding Fathers of American nationhood, which one must embrace to be a "real American." While the Founders created a model for the government of a democratic republic and abiding institutions that have made that model durable, this hardly implies that all Americans must possess a menu of the same character traits. If there is a core Americanness, over the centuries it has come to reside in a live-and-let-live commitment to a combination of diversity and support for a constantly debated, unwritten American creed comprising practical principles for getting along in daily life amid the pursuit of individual opportunity, and for maintaining a social system that balances liberty, justice, and order. One of that creed's tenets has been the freedom to maintain a distinctive cultural identity, while adopting the common behaviors and attitudes needed to attain prosperity and security and be an engaged citizen.

When immigrants have reflected on the charge that they are not real Americans, it has been a source of considerable confusion. All around them has been a diversity of peoples, manners, mores, origins, memories, and experiences. Who are the real Americans, and where does one find them? How long does it take to be admitted to their ranks? What qualifies one for admission? Who superintends that admission? As these nebulous questions indicate, it is ultimately a frustrating discussion that easily lapses into exasperation or bigotry. It is legitimate to debate how many immigrants should be admitted, but quite another matter to sort out people by ascribed characteristics that predict whether they will possess or lack an essence that is somehow "American." Yet this tendency is present throughout the American experience of immigration, especially when significant cultural and racial differences are perceived.

These assumptions about both ethnicity and authentic Americanness have produced a fear-ridden mentality that underestimates the capacities of American society to form a nation out of so many distinctive groups. Immigrants pursue opportunity, and America has long been a place for realizing that possibility. The dynamic engine that has been the American economy—combined with the constitutional framework of rights protecting an individual's citizenship and possession of property—has been both a magnet for immigrants and a guarantor of their willingness to adopt common American behaviors and attitudes. Immigrants utilize the resources at hand, whether within themselves, their families, and their ethnic groups or society, to acquire education, skills, and credentials, while pursuing better-paying employment and improved living standards. They adopt behaviors and attitudes that advance their goals, such as learning

English, the language of American opportunity. In doing so, they not only improve themselves, but they also simultaneously assimilate into American society, as they understand it. Assimilation has been aided not only by American prosperity, but also by a gradually widening national mainstream that has accommodated these aspirations. The mainstream is that societal location where individuals find access to all the resources—work, a place of residence, education, and rights under law—that make possible security and a viable standard of living. Access to the mainstream is facilitated by laws and institutional rules that have increasingly come to guarantee equality in the competition for resources. To seek inclusion in that mainstream is to put oneself in a position to assimilate, whether or not that is a conscious goal. "Assimilation is something that frequently enough happens to people," say the sociologists Richard Alba and Victor Nee, principal theorists of the mainstream concept, "while they are making other plans."

Assimilation is not a one-way street for the newcomer, but is rather, over time, a process of mutual accommodation among all elements of society. Features of individual ethnic groups are not easily found at the public level. It is not possible to say with confidence what is Italian or Chinese or Mexican or Jewish about America. Instead, it is diversity itself, in the sense of accommodating cultural and identificational differences, that is embedded in America. To be sure, the most visible accommodations are those made by immigrants, but society itself has continually been changed by the presence of diversity. All individuals, and the groups to which they belong, may bring to this mainstream distinctive identities, memories, and histories that inform behavior and understanding, so that in the process of cultural and social homogenization as people pursue opportunity, individual Americans nonetheless remain heterogeneous in their conception of who they are. A national statement of faith,

E pluribus unum (Out of many, one), appears on American money, the ultimate symbol of American opportunity. The motto is true enough, but paradoxically only as long as the observer does not expect the many to disappear as they become one or the one to look exactly the same from one historical era to another.

Chapter 6
The widening mainstream

In the early twentieth century, Henry Ford sponsored citizenship and language classes at his Michigan automobile factories, which depended heavily on immigrant labor. The climactic moment in the graduation ceremony is telling. Individual immigrant workers, with placards around their necks or small flags in their hands identifying their homelands, mounted the stage and walked into a giant wooden kettle labeled "melting pot." After emerging on the other side of the kettle, the placard or flag was gone, and each held a small American flag in his hand. They were now Americans.

Around the same time, the University of Chicago sociologists William I. Thomas and Florian Znaniecki, who were pioneers along with their Chicago colleagues in the academic study of immigrants, offered an explanation for why such a ceremony was based on simplistic, wishful thinking. They found that immigrants developed their own group life and identities and that all efforts, well-meaning or malign, to speed them rapidly into an assimilation that effaced their pasts were doomed to fail, because they were conceived outside the immigrants' experiences and needs. They wrote in the midst of a political climate in which large numbers of native-stock Americans demanded immigrants' political and cultural conformity in the name of "Americanization." Americanization might mean the suppression of foreign language newspapers, as many local and state governments demanded

9. The graduation ceremony at the Ford automobile factory English School, in which the graduates entered a simulated melting pot, often holding flags or having placards around their necks that identified their native lands, and emerged holding American flags.

during World War I, or it might mean the generally benign efforts of employers, school teachers, and social workers to teach American manners and beliefs alongside the English language.

Whatever the form of such cultural instruction, the two sociologists believed it would probably, at best, have only a superficial influence on immigrant identities. At worst, if insensitively enforced and accompanied by derision for the immigrants' cultures, it might create resistance to assimilation and animosity toward Americanizers.

Documented in what became a classic study of Polish immigration, as well as a template for understanding the resettlement problems of modern voluntary immigrants, their assumptions were based on understandings of how human beings confront all-encompassing transformations that shake the foundations of their world. In the midst of the social disorganization and individual demoralization that came with leaving the land, emigrating, and resettling in the American industrial cities, these immigrants created "a new society," neither completely Polish nor completely American. Its purpose was mutual support, consolation, and continuity in the midst of the struggles to fulfill material aspirations. Like the immigrants of the past and those entering the country alongside the Poles, they formed an *ethnic group*, with its own institutions, such as churches and mutual aid societies; informal social networks based upon family, neighborhood, and community; and an identity based on common experience, memory, language, and history.

In light of its elemental, sustaining functions, ethnicity has been a phenomenon common to all immigrant groups. While the most racialized voluntary immigrant groups, such as the Chinese, Japanese, and Mexicans, had their cultures disrupted by prejudice, legal and social discrimination, and violence, within their enclave communities they created their ethnic groups with many of the same functions one might observe among peoples who were more readily accepted. Efforts to interfere with both the group and individual processes of ethnicity were, and remain, more or less futile. People cannot live successfully, in comfort with themselves or others, without some continuity of self-understanding, personal relations, and sources of self-worth. Would the result then be an America where people could not know one another and in which revered institutions of government and society could not function? Would Americans become strangers in their own land? Not according to Thomas and Znaniecki and other University of Chicago sociologists, for they were the sources of the understanding of assimilation as not simply a process of the immigrants becoming Americans, but ultimately of mutual accommodation, in which society changes alongside the changing individuals and groups that compose it.

Immigrant accommodation has taken place at the individual, group, and institutional levels. Little that immigrants do after leaving their homelands can realistically be construed as wholly foreign. Especially in the necessary daily acts of working, creating residential arrangements, and functioning in commercial and employment markets, immigrants must learn new rules and new behaviors. Immigrant-generation parents often struggle to master these new ways; their self-transformation is rendered more difficult, because it must be accomplished in adulthood. In contrast, their American-raised children learn them more easily, though not without occasional pain, both at school, which has been the central site for formal socialization in modern society and informally, in the community among peers. School teaches an official version of American society, while the community conveys the rules for coexisting and gaining leverage in ordinary interactions.

Ethnicity may mask this process of accommodation by highlighting difference, but ethnicity has not only been about preserving an old identity. It also has been a central agent of assimilation, because the ethnic group is among the principal sites for absorbing the new rules and behaviors necessary for immigrants to fulfill their aspirations. Within the ethnic group, learning American ways by taking instruction from fellow ethnics has occurred with less pressure, ridicule, and rejection, and hence fewer penalties and less humiliation for being an inadequate student. Immigrants also have learned lessons from longer-resident ethnic groups. In this role the Irish loom especially large in historical memory, because they were relatively slow to prosper and lived longer in the proletarian neighborhoods receiving recently arrived immigrants. Their length of American residence made the Irish veterans in the processes of ethnicity and assimilation, and assisted them, along with their knowledge of English, in obtaining political power at the neighborhood and municipal levels. In the eyes of newcomers, they possessed authority about getting along in America. Ironically, the Irish embodied America for many newcomers.

The lessons learned have not been the official formulations of American values and ways. They contain much practical realism about class inequalities of power and wealth, as well as the ordinary corruptions and inefficiencies of government. They constitute recognition that for all the bright promises America offers, one must never trust that it is everything patriots say about it.

Individuals seeking opportunity

Ethnic fiction has long developed narratives that portray these transitions. In such stories of immigrant experience as Mario Puzo's *The Fortunate Pilgrim* (1964), Pietro DiDonato's *Christ in Concrete* (1939), Abraham Cahan's *The Rise of David Levinsky* (1917), Anzia Yezierska's *Bread Givers* (1925), and Amy Tan's *The Joy Luck Club* (1989), the same themes reappear, from male or female perspectives and across group lines. Informed by the authors' personal experiences as immigrants or as the American-born children of immigrants, these narratives relate to a common theme: the aspirations for a liberated self, given hope by American opportunities, but frustrated by the constraints of poverty and Old World traditions rendered dysfunctional in a new land. Often associated with the difficulties in realizing this aspiration is a conflict between parents who defend tradition and children who seek to embrace the future.

The fictional characters move painfully toward finding a place for themselves within America. It is not necessarily the place they had aspired to, as in the case of DiDonato's Paul, a sensitive young man with intellectual yearnings for truths beyond the consolations of his mother's peasant Catholic piety. He must work a construction job after his father's death in a work accident. His hopes for attaining an education are snatched from him by the family burdens he must assume. They may also find that what they thought they aspired to turns out to be hollow, as in the case of Cahan's David Levinsky, who wants to be rich, uses American opportunities to become so, and is disappointed that it does not make him happy. Or, as in the case of Puzo's Octavia, Yezierska's Sarah, and Tan's Chinese daughters, they may transform themselves into independent American women, only to find that a complete break with the past is neither possible nor desirable. But to the extent these fictional characters consider it their right to transform themselves, they represent the energies born of American opportunities.

Often lacking as a plot element are struggles by the major characters against prejudice and discrimination. This is hardly because prejudice and discrimination have been absent. For the immigrants, social acceptance and a full range of opportunities came more grudgingly than the chance to make a living at a low-wage job and tentatively to set down roots. But strategies for dealing with whatever forces limited opportunity, without having to challenge them directly from a position of relative weakness, seem always to have been available to individuals and were often successful in providing at least partial relief. If barred from skilled building trades by anti-Semitic discrimination, as they were in a number of cities, Jews had other avenues of opportunity in small business, owning corner grocery stores and discount clothing stores. They had an ethnic niche in the garment industry, in which Jews owned firms that used Jewish subcontractors and hired coethnic labor. All apparel-making businesses, independent of the owner's ethnic identity, looked for experienced, skilled pressers, sewing machine operators, and fancy stitch makers, who were widely found among immigrant Jews.

Enclave economies also provided opportunity for the Chinese, who faced significant employment discrimination. They, too, developed their own niche in the apparel industry. They also profited from the exoticization of American Chinatowns, in which they opened restaurants, bars, nightclubs, and brothels for non-Chinese consumers and employed their own people to work in them. In contrast to such urban employment niches, the Japanese in western states created a space for themselves in vegetable and fruit farming and landscaping, in which they founded successful small enterprises, using family labor and wage labor from their own ethnic group. Barred from owning land by discriminatory legislation, these immigrants often arranged to have their property placed in the legal control of their American-born children, who were citizens at birth. Their ownership might survive internment during World War II, though local officials sometimes destroyed records proving ownership, and neighbors entrusted with guardianship took advantage of the situation to seize property.

A key question for understanding assimilation is whether such ethnic niches might become a permanent trap. This did not happen. Later generations did not wish to enter these occupations, which seemed parochial, limiting, and embodiments of ethnic stereotypes they wished to shed in order to become more American. While they might provide security, they paid relatively poorly and offered fewer chances for advancement. In the twentieth century, strategies were devised, often employing education, to enter public employment, the professions, or corporate business. When they encountered discrimination in admissions to private higher educational institutions, they turned to public colleges, universities, and professional schools. The number of these public institutions grew greatly after 1945 to accommodate millions of World War II veterans, who took advantage of generous government programs to obtain higher education, and later, the postwar baby boom generation. While discrimination might be encountered in private-sector job markets, government served as a substitute, especially as the role in society of the state, at all levels, expanded in the immediate postwar decades. Federal government programs subsidized the acquisition of single-family housing and made it affordable for many to leave crowded older neighborhoods for the emerging urban fringe areas.

The barriers presented by discrimination also appeared increasingly permeable in the private sector. The American economy expanded so dramatically after 1945 that significant shortages of skilled, educated, and credentialed workers were present everywhere. With opportunity widely available, the old ethnic and religious prejudices born of competitive anxieties were gradually relaxed, along with the old barriers to mutual accommodation. Indeed, for millions of European ethnics, the types of discrimination they often encountered in the immediate postwar decades, in private businessmen's clubs, golf clubs, and resort hotels, and also in suburban housing markets, were artifacts of their growing prosperity. They were efforts to impede upwardly mobile people from making their presence felt in places where they had been absent. Those barriers, too, eventually greatly declined, and where social acceptance lagged, individuals often chose not to care, protected by ethnicity and the force of their own ambitions. They might also adopt such "passing" strategies as name changes and false family histories.

Yet the American mainstream itself widened greatly in the second half of the twentieth century. Common enrollment in public colleges and universities, and common residence in the suburbs, created new, shared patterns of life among diverse peoples. Of key importance, too, was a national self-examination spurred by various civil rights movements based on race and various liberation movements based on gender, sexual orientation, and disability. The circle of "We" in conceiving of the identity of Americans widened significantly. Passing soon became an embarrassing remnant of self-hatred. By the 1970s ethnic origins were being celebrated and publicly asserted. Immigrant peoples who had been read out of history were now being credited with significant contributions, such as the critical role Chinese railroad laborers played in building the transcontinental railroad. Historic wrongs were admitted and official apologies rendered. In 1988 President Ronald Reagan signed legislation apologizing for Japanese internment and appropriating more than $1.6 billion in reparations for those interned or their heirs.

Institutions come to embody diversity: labor unions and electoral politics

The widening mainstream was also the result of processes through which ethnic groups *as groups*, and hence diversity itself, came to be integrated into American society. Without an ancient feudal inheritance to guide its passage into modernity, the United States was invented from the ground up, especially when it came to the relationship among its diverse peoples. This is evident in electoral politics and the labor movement, both of which highlight ways in which American social processes and institutions were shaped in the nineteenth and twentieth centuries around accommodating difference.

The American labor movement has been a tentative achievement. It was slow historically to organize and to win employer recognition. It is vulnerable in the current age of globalization, because of the erosion of employment among its members as overseas and domestic nonunion competition undercut the mass production industries of the mid-twentieth century. Organized labor reached the height of its power in the decade after World War II, during which the federal government encouraged unionization for the sake of efficient war production, and approximately 36 percent (14.5 million) of American workers were unionized. While smaller than the percentage of organized workers in other advanced capitalist democracies at the time, organized labor nonetheless had substantial influence and power in politics and the industrial economy, especially in such key sectors as garments, consumer electronics, household appliances, automobiles, steel, rubber, and chemicals. It was a dependable part of the Democratic coalition that controlled national politics between the 1930s and the 1970s and that successfully advanced a social democratic program for government. With job losses in basic industries after 1980, as the fortunes of organized labor declined—about 14.7 million employees (11.9 percent) were unionized late in 2010—so, too, did the Democratic Party. These numbers nonetheless belie organized labor's contemporary importance, for it is especially prominent in the dynamic government, education, and healthcare sectors.

The tentativeness of American labor unionism's achievements has many causes, but one that looms especially large historically, alongside the diversity of the economy and the size of the country, is the cultural diversity of the workforce. Immigrants understood the value of solidarity. Ethnic group formation was premised on collective action in such endeavors as forming churches and synagogues and sectarian school systems (for Catholics, Lutherans, and Orthodox Jews) as alternatives to state-funded schools. Large numbers of immigrant workers, especially the nineteenth-century English, Scots, and Germans, had already experienced class conflict, radical politics, and union organizational campaigns born of protests against proletarianization during the Industrial Revolution in Europe. But while many experiences taught the value of solidarity, immigration was ultimately based on individual initiative and individual and family aspirations. During the most sustained formation of mass production industries, immigrant workers were enabled by the revolution in transoceanic transportation to make money and quickly return home. Organizing campaigns and prolonged strikes were an impediment to these aspirations. When provoked by employer actions such as reneging on wage agreements, even these birds of passage might react with a job action. But these short spasms of militancy could not create a labor movement.

Thus, though immigration was about material rewards, it did not necessarily inspire worker solidarity in their pursuit. Observing immigrant behavior, unions saw most immigrants as unorganizable and an impediment to labor's progress. Furthermore, most unions in the late nineteenth and early twentieth centuries represented skilled craft workers. In contrast, the immigrants were mostly unskilled workers, such as machine tenders on assembly lines or outdoor construction laborers. If they worked in the same industries with skilled unionized workers, they were not represented by their unions and certainly did not share their wage scales. Unions of skilled workers also were, by and large, made up of native-stock white workers and long-resident northern and western European ethnics. A good deal of nativist contempt for foreigners frequently informed their response to recent eastern, central, and southern European immigrants—people of dubious whiteness, who seemed willing to take any sort of abuse to make a dollar. Asians, Mexicans, African Americans, and other nonwhites inspired even greater hostility. The occasional use of immigrant workers as strikebreakers hardened the view that immigrants were poor union material.

What was needed was a new union movement, which simultaneously reached out to all workers and organized workers by industry, not by skill level, in the interests of both collective power and countering the use of immigrants to break strikes and wage scales. Skilled workers, too, knew that they could be replaced by a new machine worked by an unskilled immigrant, especially if the latter felt no sense of moral obligation to them and was not bound by union discipline.

The impediments to the development of this sort of unionism were many, not the least of them being the distrust among ethnic groups and the power of employers when supported, as they frequently were, by state power in the form of both court injunctions against striking unions and the use of state militias and federal troops to protect strikebreakers and break picket lines. Yet gradually during the first half of the twentieth century, in one mass production industry after another, unions with strong multiethnic, and ultimately multiracial, foundations were formed.

These unions did not deny cultural differences but respected them and balanced them off against a common commitment to aspirational, working-class American values of fairness, equality, and class solidarity. While immigrant and ethnic workers, such as Mexican and Filipino agricultural laborers and Chinese, Jewish, and Italian garment workers, showed considerable initiative in organization campaigns when encouraged to participate, leadership in union organizing often came from the more class-conscious elements of American and older ethnic group workers, who were the veterans of past struggles. Walter and Victor Reuthen, the sons of German immigrant socialists, spent their lives in the labor movement and were instrumental in the formation of the multiethnic, multiracial United Auto Workers. A similar evolution toward inclusiveness may be traced in the United Steelworkers of America, whose founder and first president, Philip Murray, was born in Scotland, and in the United Rubber Workers, whose first president, Sherman Dalrymple, a native-born Anglo-American, was raised on a West Virginia farm. Equitable apportioning of union offices and leadership positions in the workplace on negotiation committees and as shop stewards was proof of union leaders' willingness to recognize immigrant workers. Thus, labor unionism, a vital element of American social democracy, emerged out of multicultural foundations. It continues to do so in the twenty-first century. After internal debates that closely resembled those of the past, sectors of the American labor movement have once again become committed to organizing immigrant workers, such as the large numbers of women employed in housekeeping by corporate hotel chains and as healthcare workers in nursing and assisted-living facilities.

A similar evolution took place in electoral politics, though much more rapidly. The stakes in American elections, especially at local levels, have always been greater than the prestige of the offices contested, because the victor has taken control of public resources, especially government jobs, that might be apportioned to friends, family, and electoral supporters. Self-conscious heirs of the Founding Fathers, native white Americans rarely saw it that way, believing elections were not about opportunity, but about principles interpreted by individual conscience. Early in the history of American elections, however, as the electorate swelled beyond the narrow ranks of substantial property holders through the democratization of the franchise in individual states, politicians came to understand that political patronage in the form of jobs was a useful tool in mobilizing plebian supporters.

They also came to understand that it was impossible to mobilize a mass electorate one voter at a time. What was needed was a way of approaching the voters as members of groups with their own leaders, who might become clients of politicians and power brokers in their own right. From the arrival of the Irish Catholics, Germans, and various groups of Scandinavians in the mid-nineteenth century, political parties came to see the advantage of mobilizing ethnic leadership and voters to form electoral majorities. The numbers of immigrants seemed endless, and after only five years of American residence, they were entitled to become citizens and to vote. For their part, ethnics proved disciplined voters—if offered incentives. Solidarity in electoral politics came easier to the immigrants and their descendants than it did to Anglo-Americans, whose belief in principled individualism made them slower to recognize group interests. Ethnic groups voted undeviatingly for the party of their choice, often for many decades. Scandinavians were longtime Republicans. Irish Americans were Democratic loyalists and party leaders at every level for well over a century. Jews have been among the most solidly Democratic of the white ethnic groups for decades. A significant majority of Florida Cubans have been solidly Republican for decades. Superimposed on these ethnic preferences has been a succession process, by which each new wave of immigration has contested for power with the previous ones in positions of party leadership.

In return for votes, politicians have promised a variety of symbolic recognitions and concrete benefits. In addition to nominations to office and public employment, there has been assistance to communities in the form of such social services as neighborhood public schools, police protection, public health programs, and parks and recreational facilities. The gradual progress of civil service reform led to apportioning most public employment through objective measures of fitness determined by job experience and performance on standardized tests, which undercut patronage politics. Yet ethnic bases for mobilizing the American electorate abide, because politics still apportions a variety of resources and recognitions along partisan lines.

Another long-standing function of ethnic politics has concerned homeland affairs, and because it is transnational in its reach, it has always been especially controversial to the extent that concern for a homeland could be construed as indifference to America. As a source of controversy, however, it, too, suggests the mutual accommodations by which American pluralism has been formed. Among these homeland issues have been not only demands for changes in immigration restrictions and support for increased numbers of refugees, but also matters directly involving American foreign policy, such as support for opposition to international aggression or for homeland liberation, or offering aid to victims of communal violence in homelands. There is a long list of instances in which pressure has been exerted through the power of ethnic votes and campaign contributions. These efforts emerged first among the Irish. Soon after attaining significant numbers in politics in the 1850s, they organized on behalf of American support for the liberation of Ireland from British rule. An Irish campaign about homeland affairs continued through the creation of the Irish Free State in 1921 and the independent Republic of Ireland in 1949 and would ultimately include the question of control of Northern Ireland and support for Catholic rights protests there in the late twentieth century.

The Irish have not been alone in using their vote and the possession of free speech and the right to organize as a wedge to influence American law and policy. Poles, Czechs, and Slovaks wanted support for independent homelands before and during World War I. During the Cold War, a wide variety of eastern and central European ethnics pressured the American government to free their homelands from Soviet control. Jews sought but were largely unsuccessful in influencing American refugee policy in the 1930s in an effort to obtain more visas for those seeking to flee Germany. After the creation of Israel in 1948, they began a decades-long effort on behalf of government support for Israel's security. To combat that effort, Arab Americans, whose numbers have grown since 1965, mobilized their votes behind politicians sympathetic to Palestinians. Italian Americans, in the two decades after World War II, organized to obtain increases in the admission of Italian immigrants and refugees above quota levels. Since the Cuban Revolution of 1959, Cuban Americans have used their large numbers in Florida to influence refugee policy and to support an economic boycott of Cuba.

This transnational ethnic politics has been criticized on the grounds that the groups involved manifest disloyalty—or sometimes, more generously stated, unresolved dual loyalties. Yet such activism has drawn ethnic groups into the mainstream, while widening it to legitimize their presence and concerns. The Irish became more American in substantial measure through decades of advocacy for their homeland, and the same dynamic process can be seen among more recently arrived peoples such as Vietnamese, Tibetans, and Rwandans. When criticized by Americans for conflicted loyalties, Irish Americans justified their activism by saying they were demonstrating their *American* patriotism. They explained that the ideal situation for a liberated Ireland would be for it to adopt the values and institutional models of the American polity. Involvement in the processes of politics, moreover, integrated the Irish further into the political party system and taught them to present their issues to those outside their group and make use of the institutions of government. It is no contradiction in the minds of Irish Americans that their St. Patrick's Day parades have routinely given representation simultaneously to symbols of both American loyalty and Irish nationalism.

Across the continent, the same phenomenon manifested itself in the San Francisco area in the 1930s and 1940s, as Chinese Americans assumed a public role as advocates for China in its struggle against Japanese aggression. Voting was of less consequence than among the Irish, because there were far fewer Chinese citizens, and they were concentrated in a small number of electoral districts. But through large, well-planned public rallies, parades, and demonstrations, they influenced American policy and public opinion. Chinese American women worked through their labor union, the Independent Ladies' Garment Workers' Union, to organize a boycott of Japanese goods. During the war, they joined the American women's armed forces in significant numbers in order to play a role in defeating Japan.

These examples of cohesive pluralism demonstrate the power of ethnicity simultaneously to strengthen the group and to assist it in speeding its way into the mainstream. America has not always enthusiastically welcomed immigrants. But its homogenizing social and political arrangements create opportunities to become a part of an American society that is more unified, and hence stronger, because of the integration of diverse peoples, who retain their differences even as they come to act and think in common.

Chapter 7
The future of assimilation

Because significant American institutions have been shaped around accommodating difference, the absorptive capacities of American society have been formidable. Yet some observers believe those powers are receding and that the current mass immigration is speeding their demise. Among the most influential has been the political scientist Samuel P. Huntington (1927–2008). If present immigration trends continue, America will lose what Huntington believed to be its "core Anglo-Protestant culture," which, he argued, has made it uniquely successful among nations and has been the source of political stability. Bereft of its unifying identity, America will then suffer cultural Balkanization and perhaps eventually physical fragmentation. Huntington echoed the nativism of a century ago, but he was quick to attempt to separate himself from its racialized bigotry. America does not need "Anglo-Protestants" to survive, he maintained, but rather the public culture they created. Creed, not genes, will determine its future. Immigrants in the past remade themselves in the image of Anglo-Protestantism, while those today refuse to do so, and in a political climate enamored by the vision of a postnational, globalized world order, they are not required to do so. For Huntington, the greatest threat to the continuity of America as a democratic republic lay in recent immigrants, who seemed to him to be unenthusiastic about assuming the responsibilities of American citizenship.

This pessimistic vision rests on faulty but hardly uncommon assumptions. For Huntington, American public culture, Anglo-Protestantism, as reflected in the nation's laws, system of governance, and social values, seems frozen in time, unchanging in its essence since the dawn of the United States. With its hunger for an idealized, much simplified past, such an argument defies the logic of the modern world, with its ceaseless pace of change. No place, however once remote, has been free from being swept along by such transformations. A half century after the American Revolution, the United States had already begun its transformation from the underpopulated, provincial society of citizen farmers, artisans, and slave-owning planters into an urban, industrial world power. As early as the 1840s, that transformation began to be reflected in the frequent remaking of the American workforce and American institutions, such as political parties, by immigration. Multicultural diversity is constitutive of the processes of change, and hence of American society itself.

To be sure, for Huntington the contemporary failure of assimilation is based on a substantive historical transition in the character of immigrants who, he assumed, are no longer required to, and increasingly do not care to, assimilate. Unlike past immigrants, they do not want to be a part of America. They go back and forth across borders, especially the porous Mexican border, with little concern for the problems or future of American society. The formal exercise of citizenship is irrelevant to them.

There are indeed those present-day immigrants who, like the birds of passage of the past, have no intention of resettling permanently and may be charged, just as those migrants were a century ago, with using the United States as a cash machine. Yet this familiar charge overlooks, as it did in the past, the value of the work they do while they are in the United States, which from the practical standpoint of most lawmakers is why they have been encouraged to migrate. The international search for opportunity is easier than it was a century ago, because of the rapid pace of economic globalization and technological change in transportation and communication. Moreover, as in the past but on an even broader scale, governments, including that of the United States, encourage transnationality by recognizing dual citizenships and easing the transfer of money, property, and capital between homelands and lands of resettlement.

In the scale and ease of such itinerancy, the world may indeed be a different place than it was during the previous population movements that critics of contemporary immigration find did not challenge the Anglo-Protestant culture they revere—although one could never have convinced the nativists of the past that those immigrations were not cause for alarm. Nation-states will probably never again reside in isolation from the moment-to-moment workings of world labor and capital markets. There is equally little doubt that itinerant workers, managers, and entrepreneurs, with cosmopolitan attitudes that leave them more or less indifferent to the history and memory of the places in which they reside for material gain, will be present in unprecedented numbers everywhere there is opportunity, whether in Dubai, Shanghai, Rio de Janeiro, or Chicago. On the other hand, American immigration law continues to encourage the reconstruction of families. The children of these immigrant families grow up in a new society, attend its schools, and form their peer groups in their neighborhoods and schools. America is the only world they know. Throughout the history of American immigration, a common impediment to the re-emigration of immigrant parents has been the disposition of their children to continue to live the only life they know—an American life. When immigrant parents take these children to their ancestral homeland for a visit in order to acquaint them with its culture, language, and landscape, the result is that the children often come to a conscious understanding of just how American they are.

Thus, fundamental elements of their situation, such as a well-paying job, homeownership, and parenting of Americanizing children, work to direct even those immigrants inclined to return to their homelands toward assimilation. Assimilation has never been simply a matter of the formal oaths of the naturalization process or about assuming or declining an identity. Immigrants and their children must involve themselves in socioeconomic processes that move them and their families toward the mainstream, for it is in their interest to learn American behaviors and attitudes in pursuing their own aspirations.

Significant questions have been raised about whether the daily social and economic processes of assimilation that direct immigrants and their children into the mainstream are working as effectively as in the past. One set of concerns legitimately arises out of the volume of illegal immigration, which flows largely from Mexico and Central America. Unauthorized immigrants encounter the threat of legal prosecution that imperils their ability to reside and work in the United States, inhibits property ownership and family security, and weakens their ability to attain wage equality with legal residents. While there has always been illegal immigration, numbers in the early twenty-first century, perhaps as many as 13 million between 2010 and 2020, dwarf anything thought to have previously existed. Many employers have come to depend on this source of cheap labor and employ it to free themselves from the burden of paying the mandated minimum wage, negotiating with unions, and meeting the costs of such worker benefits as health insurance. Moreover, unauthorized immigrants, as consumers and taxpayers, have become significant, as workers, consumers, and taxpayers, to local and regional economies. Even in a state like Ohio, far from the nation's southern border and not a major destination for immigrants (about 4.3 percent of population in 2014), has a significant investment in unauthorized workers. A study in that year by the Immigration Policy Center estimated that the state's economy would lose up to $83 million a year in state and local taxes if unauthorized immigrants were removed. Ohio DACA recipients, the Dreamers, were estimated to account for $14.1 million in state and local taxes in 2016. In Colorado, with an immigrant population of 10 percent, unauthorized immigrants are estimated by the same organization to have paid $139.5 million in state and local taxes in 2015 and DACA recipients to have paid $34 million. Some of these taxes paid by the undocumented help fund programs that they are barred by law from using. In comparison, the equivalent figures for states such as New York and California, with much larger immigrant populations, are billions of dollars annually.

This morally and politically untenable situation breeds exploitation and profound inequalities, strains law enforcement, and fosters contempt for law. Options for resolving it include guest-worker programs, tougher and consistently enforced employer penalties for hiring illegal immigrants, enhanced border security, and an expedited path to citizenship for those unauthorized immigrants who desire it. Political paralysis has blocked and continues to block action. The issue involves border security in an age of international terrorism, the bilateral relations between Mexico and the United States, the prosperity of important industries, the livelihoods of American workers, and the appearance of tolerance for lawbreaking. It carries practical, symbolic, and emotional weight, with political risks for those who seek to resolve it.

If illegal immigration were successfully addressed, it would still be necessary to confront another set of concerns: Are the relevant social and economic processes leading immigrants into the mainstream working successfully for the majority—the legal contemporary immigrants—whose ranks the former illegals might then join? Did these same processes work evenly and invariably in the past? If the contemporary situation is indeed unprecedented and beyond American experience, it may be a cause for despair. For cultural conservatives like Huntington, the key to their prediction that immigrants will not assimilate lies in cultural differences that will inevitably breed disorder.

Analysts on the Left, who are sympathetic to the immigrants, are interested in equality and social justice more than in social order. But they, too, see a threat to assimilation. What is crucial for their analysis is the question of racism. Today's immigrants are largely nonwhite in a society in which race has been a significant marker of privilege. When combined with the tentativeness of contemporary, postindustrial job markets for launching successful, secure lives, will limitations of opportunity combine with racist prejudices and discrimination to deny immigrants and their children access to the mainstream and doom them to permanent poverty and social marginality? Such observers have ventured to project that, if so, many immigrants will experience a different type of assimilation—a downward, segmented assimilation. Rather than upward mobility, they will fall permanently into the urban underclass, residing in the crime-infested, drug-ridden ghetto-slums of decaying inner cities, which they will share with poor African Americans. They will make money on the wrong side of the law for want of alternatives, or they will depend on expensive, tax-supported social assistance programs, which contemporary local and state governments can no longer afford and taxpayers do not wish to subsidize.

Testing pessimistic scenarios

Nightmare scenarios aside, historic assimilation patterns have been analyzed in a number of studies based on massive sets of quantitative data and, most importantly, a variety of systematic comparisons, using comparable historical and contemporary data, between ethnic groups in the past and those in the present. Joel Perlmann, one of the most thorough of these investigators, and other researchers have summarized the results of these investigations:

1. As in the past, there are differences among and within the contemporary immigrant groups, so it is not possible to generalize about the category "immigrant."

2. Not all contemporary immigrants are poor and bring low skill sets; a substantial number possess academic and technical education and job skills when they arrive in the United States.

3. While high-wage, machine-tender factory jobs are in shorter supply than at the time of the second great immigration, lower-skill work, including factory employment, exists in sufficient volume to employ many unskilled immigrants with steady work in times of economic prosperity.

4. Just as was true for many of the children of the second-wave immigrants in the early twentieth century, educational advancement continues to support upward mobility. A number of contemporary immigrant groups have used education for credentialing and thus have attained stability in white- and blue-collar jobs.

5. Racial hierarchies are socially and culturally formed and, as in the past, evolve and dissolve over time. Many European immigrants were racialized and entered the mainstream, and America's visible minorities (African American, Hispanic, Native American, and Asian American) have unprecedented access to the mainstream today, though structural inequities certainly abide, especially for poor African Americans.

6. Crime among youth of immigrant families, and types of segmented assimilation more generally, are hardly new phenomena and, where they have been common, they have not proven permanent.

As in the past, there is variability in the experiences of contemporary individuals and immigrant groups, with some achieving stability and prosperity, but some not doing as well. There are those who find themselves, like the Italians of the first half of the twentieth century, accused of failing to assimilate, being mired in poverty and crime, and taxing law-enforcement agencies and social services. It is easy to forget the fear about blocked mobility that attached itself especially to the urban, working-class Italian immigrants and their American-raised children and thus inspired such pessimistic sociological studies as

William Foote Whyte's *Street Corner Society: The Social Structure of an Italian Slum* (1943). Whyte reported on life in a neighborhood judged by respectable Americans to be, as his publisher said in marketing the book, "mysterious, dangerous, and depressing." Some young men dropped out of school, worked irregularly, joined gangs, participated in petty or serious crime, and had troubled relations with police. Other young men, whose lifestyle was less colorful, left school for the industrial workforce, just as young women left school to become wives and mothers. There are few traces of this inner-city, white, working-class ethnic world left today. Instead, there are some newer immigrants who might be described in the same way.

For Perlmann and others, the critical test case for the possibility that contemporary immigrants will find the mainstream in ways that are historically conventional or will, alternatively, fall victim to downward, segmented assimilation lies in the trajectory of the largest group of contemporary immigrants, Mexicans, with whom the United States is fated to share a singular relationship. Because of the educational credentials, job skills, savings, and tight family and community solidarity many Asians bring to the United States, they are deemed less problematic. Some analysts, in fact, project a new, polarized racial hierarchy forming in which Asians join whites of European background at the top of the racial pyramid, and immigrants from the Caribbean, Africa, and Latin America, especially Mexicans, will be positioned at various levels toward or at the bottom.

Mexicans are also critical to the pessimism of contemporary nativists, who predict that rather than the Americanization of Mexican immigrants, what will evolve in the twenty-first century is the Hispanicization of America, largely because the Mexicans cannot and will not assimilate. The source of this pessimism is a conjunction of related situational factors and political, economic, and social processes. The long land border between the United

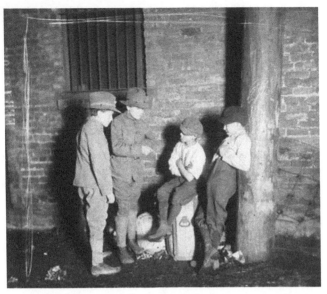

10. **Long considered resistant to assimilation, Italian immigrants, like these young street boys, were frequently the targets of Americanizers. As the cued body language of both sets of boys suggests, this photograph seems to have been posed for an American audience of newspaper readers who accepted that view of Italians.**

States and Mexico facilitates a continuing high volume of legal and illegal immigration; Mexicans are concentrated in especially high numbers in southwestern states along that border; and the desire of Mexicans to enter the United States has shown no signs of abating significantly, mainly because of the uneven performance of the Mexican economy. Supplemented by constant migrations, Mexicans might well create a world of their own inside the United States. Moreover, Huntington's research suggested to him that Mexican assimilation lags in language shift, education beyond the primary grades, occupational and income mobility, intermarriage, American identification, and citizenship acquisition.

At the end of this nightmare scenario is a restive, disloyal, and unassimilated Mexican population living in isolation in the United States and acting as the subversive wedge for a Mexican irredentism focused on retaking the territory Americans conquered in the mid-nineteenth century. It is a vision that, alongside the general anxieties about the decline of the size of the white population, helps to animate nativism. It mobilizes Americanizers, who campaign for English-only policies, especially in public education, and for restrictive immigration and public welfare laws that, in turn, breed angry resistance to assimilation, especially among rebellious ethnic young people.

Yet contemporary and historical research, utilizing official government statistics and local ethnographic surveys, does not yield evidence of a unique social pathology among Mexicans that might lead to a permanent, dangerous underclass, let alone resistance to assimilation. The importance of Perlmann's research is that he simultaneously undertook systematic socioeconomic comparisons between the Italian and other European immigrants of a century ago, contemporary African Americans, and recent Mexican immigrants. Like the Italians and others, the Mexican second generation does tend to leave school early for the workforce and for homemaking, at a time when education is crucial for upward socioeconomic mobility. But Mexican American youth have relatively high labor force participation and were found to be more likely to be working full-time than American-born whites and blacks. Their income tends to be lower than that of whites because of their educational deficit, but higher than that of African Americans. Among Mexicans, relative especially to poor inner-city African Americans, the single mother/missing (or incarcerated) father household is much less prevalent. This relatively greater presence of intact families helps to explain the greater income relative to African Americans of Mexican American families in which there are working women. When Mexican Americans and native whites are at the same level of educational attainment, there is virtual parity in family income.

The policy implications of such findings are that relatively low-cost efforts encouraging high school graduation and combating job discrimination might significantly impact the prospects for more Mexican Americans joining the mainstream in a timely fashion. More time spent in school would probably increase command of English, but the language deficit is not nearly as dire as often imagined. While Mexican American educational attainment has been relatively low, the high school dropout rate is declining and college entrance increasing for Mexican American youth. In 1990 it was found that among the third generation, which is now well into adulthood, two-thirds of Mexican American families spoke only English at home. Research also revealed that the percentage of Mexican Americans in the twenty-five- to forty-four-year-old cohort able to speak English did not vary greatly whether individuals lived near the border, in a border state, or in the interior of the United States and was between 95 percent and 98 percent in all three physical locations. Since the study, based on 1990 data, many more recent Mexican immigrants have filled the country, and the processes of language acquisition began evolving for these newly relocated migrants.

But if the trend among earlier immigrants continues, as they work to attain security, education, and socioeconomic mobility, English acquisition will continue apace. Language proficiency is a complicated, relative matter. In 2017, 67 percent of Mexicans in the country self-described as having "limited English proficiency," compared to 48 percent for all immigrants, but that figure includes those who speak English "well" (as opposed to "very well") and "not very well." Immigrants, past and present, have often functioned quite effectively speaking English with an accent or a limited vocabulary or ungrammatically, as do many native-born Americans. Noteworthy, too, in sharp contrast to the historical past, is the availability of bilingual services, especially in Spanish but also in other immigrant languages, in many public and commercial contexts, and hence the significant contemporary accommodation of language diversity.

When compared to the southern, eastern, and central European immigrants of a century ago, Mexicans have been progressing more slowly, so it might take them four or five generations, rather than three or four, to close the gaps that keep them more on the margins than in the center of the mainstream, but there is nothing intrinsically Mexican about the situation. Much has to do with the larger society in which they reside and work. European immigrants of a century ago arrived at a time when income inequality was declining, but the gap between the affluent and the rest of society has been growing in America for decades. Moreover, government services to assist parts of the population in need to prepare to take advantage of opportunity are in decline. In light of these challenges, immigrant achievements in creating American roots are especially noteworthy. In 2015, 51 percent of all immigrant household heads owned their own homes; among naturalized citizens, the figure rose to 64.6 percent. For American-born household heads, homeownership was an almost precisely comparable 65.5 percent.

Such findings are not sufficient as a basis for the future of immigration policy. They do not mandate that permanent, large-scale immigration is the best policy or a poor policy. The questions of numbers and criteria for determining who will be admitted must be determined according to projections of economic growth and the social costs of supporting and maintaining the generations of Americans, whatever their origins, who will see the nation into the future. But they do indicate that the most pessimistic conclusions about the future of immigrant assimilation need not determine immigration policy, which should instead be based on constructive calculations about the economic and social interests of both Americans and immigrants. They also suggest that Americans need not consider themselves embarking into the unknown when considering contemporary immigration. They have confronted mass immigration before, and American society has not only survived but become stronger for the diversity embedded within it.

Yet these findings also suggest the depths of an ongoing crisis that is not sufficiently addressed: the stagnant position of many members of America's largest historical domestic racial minority, African Americans, who are being passed by as immigrants move into the mainstream. It remains a bitter irony in the midst of celebrations of immigrant achievements that programs, such as affirmative action in hiring or in college admissions, which were developed in the mid-twentieth century following civil rights protests to address long-standing institutional racism and to assist African Americans, have been utilized more successfully by nonwhite immigrants to speed their own entrance into the mainstream. The government has allowed the application of such programs to immigrants of color and their children in the service of the laudable goals of immigrant assimilation and multicultural diversity in workplaces and educational institutions. But the ongoing neglect of their original intentions is no credit to American social policy, and the consequences remained dramatically visible in the protest demonstrations around police treatment of African Americans in 2020.

Conclusion

Americans have built a global society whose peoples' origins look much like the world. This is an observation made daily by international visitors for whom such symbolic locations at the crossroad of American diversity as New York City's Times Square or the multicultural neighborhoods of big cities possess a cosmopolitan dynamism that seems uniquely American. At eye level these exciting manifestations of multicultural America are not easily forgotten, especially by those residing in more homogeneous societies.

This global society developed unevenly. There has never been consensus on whether it should be a national aspiration. It arose while Americans were pursuing another end: the material development of their part of North America. While American diversity certainly has been debated widely in ideological terms, at the heart of its creation was and continues to be a matter that resists moral calculation: the demand for labor to sustain economic development. Immigration has been an economic and social investment in human labor, and the cheaper the labor, the more it has been valued. A labor force formed exclusively from a native-born American population would not have been large enough to propel the United States into the status of the world's leading economy in the twentieth century. Current American population growth is the result of immigration. With an aging native-born population, there are probably not enough Americans to provide for the country's future needs for workers. Moreover, immigrants are proving vital to the renewal of American cities and, as taxpayers, to the support of government social programs.

American debates about immigration have been more complicated and emotionally fraught because the necessary (labor) and the good (homogeneity or heterogeneity) have been tied together, forming a knot that it is difficult to undo. Over time what came to exist as a result of economic calculation also came to be regarded by many as an object of pride in a way that the slave trade, another source of labor, could never be. Even those who stood against the continuation of large-scale immigration might argue that it was no longer as beneficial as it had once been, but represents a venerable history, worthy of respect, if no longer of emulation. It has frequently been noted that for many contemporary Americans, their own immigrant ancestors, however once berated by the native-born, were hard-working, right-living, God-fearing people who were ideal material for citizenship—in contrast to contemporary immigrants, whom these same Americans believe embody opposite, negative characteristics. But then the contemporary multiculturalist's own rhetorical formulation of "the real America"—a nation united in the acceptance of difference and the belief that Americans are best when they are diverse—expresses a vision that has hardly been uncontested. Nor has it been widely rejected. Public opinion polls continue to reflect sharp divisions. When Americans were asked by the Gallup polling organization in 2019 if immigration should be kept at its present levels, 35 percent said it should be decreased, 27 percent said it should be increased, and 37 percent said that the present levels were acceptable.

To be sure, the actual, frequently messy work of forming societies is quite different from the idealistic, patriotic views that come to justify and sustain them and that provide both emotionally sustaining explanations for complex developments and sources of national pride. As its immigration history and the mythologies that pass for understanding of that history make clear, America is no different in that regard. Amid these abiding contentions, where is "the real America"? This book holds out a tentative conclusion: in the sweep of its 250-year history, the evidence may yet sustain a judgment that the achievement of the United States in creating a global society is its greatest claim to emulation and respect.

Further reading

Introduction

Gerstle, Gary. *American Crucible: Race and Nation in the Twentieth Century*. Princeton, NJ: Princeton University Press, 2001.

Jacobson, Matthew Frye. *Whiteness of a Different Color: European Immigrants and the Alchemy of Race*. Cambridge, MA: Harvard University Press, 1999.

Roediger, David R. *Working toward Whiteness: How America's Immigrants Became White*. New York: Basic Books, 2005.

Part I

Hirota, Hidetaka. *Expelling the Poor: Atlantic Seaboard States and the Nineteenth Century Origins of American Immigration Policy*. New York: Oxford University Press, 2017.

Kanstroom, Daniel. *Deportation Nation: Outsiders in American History*. Cambridge, MA: Harvard University Press, 2007.

Kraut Alan M. *Silent Travelers: Germs, Genes, and the Immigrant Menace*. Baltimore: Johns Hopkins University Press, 1995.

Lee, Erika. *America for Americans: A History of Xenophobia in the United States*. New York: Basic Books, 2019.

Lee, Erika. *The Making of Asian America: A History*. New York: Simon & Schuster, 2015.

Ngai, Mae M. *Impossible Subjects: Illegal Aliens and the Making of Modern America*. Princeton, NJ: Princeton University Press, 2004.

Parker, Kunal. *Making Foreigners: Immigration and the Law of Citizenship, 1600-2000*. New York: Cambridge University Press, 2015.

Salyer, Lucy E., *Laws Harsh as Tigers: Chinese Immigrants and the Shaping of Modern Immigration Law*. Chapel Hill: University of North Carolina Press, 1995.

Wyman, Mark. *Round-Trip to America: The Immigrants Return to Europe, 1880-1930*. Ithaca, NY: Cornell University Press, 1993.

Part II

Battisti, Danielle, *Whom We Shall Welcome: Italian Americans and Immigration Reform, 1945-1965*. New York: Fordham University Press, 2019.

Baynton, Douglas C. *Defectives in the Land: Disability and Immigration in the Age of Eugenics*. Chicago: University of Chicago Press, 2016.

Bodnar, John. *The Transplanted: A History of Immigrants in Urban America*. Bloomington: Indiana University Press, 1985.

Dinnerstein, Leonard. *America and the Survivors of the Holocaust*. New York: Columbia University Press, 1982.

Foner, Nancy. *From Ellis Island to JFK: New York's Two Great Waves of Immigration*. New Haven, CT: Yale University Press, 2000.

Gardiner, Martha. *The Qualities of a Citizen: Women, Immigration, and Citizenship, 1870-1965*. Princeton, NJ: Princeton University Press, 2005.

Leavitt, Peggy. *The Transnational Villagers*. Berkeley: University of California Press, 2001.

Reimers, David. *Other Immigrants: The Global Origins of the American People*. New York: New York University Press, 2005.

Part III

Alba, Richard, and Victor Nee. *Remaking the American Mainstream: Assimilation and Contemporary Immigration*. Cambridge, MA: Harvard University Press, 2003.

Garcia, Maria Cristina. *The Refugee Challenge in Post–Cold War America*. New York: Oxford University Press, 2017.

Huntington, Samuel P. *Who Are We?: Challenges to American National Identity*. New York: Simon & Schuster, 2005.

Miller, David. *Strangers in Our Midst: The Political Philosophy of Immigration*. Cambridge, MA: Harvard University Press, 2016.

Perlmann, Joel. *Italians Then, Mexicans Now: Immigrant Origins and Second-Generation Progress, 1890–2000*. New York: Russell Sage Foundation, 2005.

Portes, Alejandro, and Reuben G. Rumbaut. *Legacies: The Story of the Immigrant Second Generation*. Berkeley: University of California Press, 2001.

Index

Note: Page numbers in *italics* signify figures or illustrations. Specific legislation is found under the heading of law and legislation.

Index

American Immigration